STATISTICAL HANDBOOK OF

JAPAN

JN116357

2022

Statistics Japan

© 2022 by Statistics Bureau
Ministry of Internal Affairs and Communications
Japan
All rights reserved.

Edited and Published by
Statistics Bureau
Ministry of Internal Affairs and Communications
Japan
19-1 Wakamatsu-cho, Shinjuku-ku
Tokyo 162-8668 Japan

Published by
Japan Statistical Association
2-4-6, Hyakunin-cho, Shinjuku-ku
Tokyo 169-0073 Japan

Printed in Japan
ISBN 978-4-8223-4159-6 C0033 ¥ 3300E

https://www.stat.go.jp/english/data/handbook/index.html

Preface

This handbook is designed to provide a clear and coherent overview of present-day Japan through statistics.

It provides statistical tables, figures, maps and photographs to portray conditions in modern-day Japan from a variety of perspectives, including demographics, economic and social trends, and culture. Most of the comments and statistical data for this purpose have been drawn from principal statistical publications available from government and other leading sources.

For more in-depth statistical information on Japan, readers are invited to peruse the Japan Statistical Yearbook.

We hope that this handbook will serve as a guide in your search for knowledge about Japan. We are always happy to receive opinions or requests from readers.

You can also view the contents of this handbook on the website of the Statistics Bureau.

September 2022

INOUE Takashi
Director-General
Statistics Bureau
Ministry of Internal Affairs
and Communications
Japan

Notes for Users

1. The present issue basically contains statistics that became available by April 30, 2022.

2. Unless otherwise indicated, "year" refers to the calendar year and "fiscal year" refers to the 12 months beginning April 1 of the year stated.

3. Metric units are used in all tables and figures in which the data are measured in weight, volume, length or area. Refer to Appendix 2 for conversion factors.

4. Unless otherwise indicated, amounts shown are in Japanese yen. Refer to Appendix 3 for exchange rates of JPY per U.S. dollar.

5. Statistical figures may not add up to the totals due to rounding.

6. The following symbols are used in the tables:

   $\cdots$ Data not available

   $-$ Magnitude zero or figures not applicable

   0 or 0.0   Less than half of unit employed

   #   Marked break in series

   *   Provisional or estimate

7. Data relating to "China" generally exclude those for Hong Kong SAR, Macao SAR and Taiwan.

8. All contents of the present issue, including tables, figures, and maps, are also available on the website:

   https://www.stat.go.jp/english/data/handbook/index.html

9. When any contents of the present issue are to be quoted or copied in other media (print or electronic), the title is to be referred to as follows:

   Source: Statistical Handbook of Japan 2022, Statistics Bureau, Ministry of Internal Affairs and Communications, Japan.

10. "Statistics Bureau, MIC" in the tables and figures is an abbreviation of "Statistics Bureau, Ministry of Internal Affairs and Communications, Japan".

Contents

List of Tables

List of Figures

Photo Sources

Cover photo: Mt.Fuji

A competitive performance of light. Every year, fireworks displays are held in the summer and winter at Lake Kawaguchi. Mt. Fuji is the highest peak in Japan, with an elevation of 3,776 meters. In June 2013, it was registered as a World Cultural Heritage Site, making it the 17th World Heritage Site in Japan.

Chapter 1

Land and Climate

© TANAKA Takayuki

Japan has four seasons, and beautiful natural scenes can be enjoyed in spring, summer, fall, and winter. In winter, there are many snowy days on the Sea of Japan side of Japan, and some places accumulate over 3 meters of snow, mainly along the mountains.

1. Land

Japan is an island country situated off the eastern seaboard of the Eurasian continent in the northern hemisphere. The islands form a crescent-shaped archipelago stretching from northeast to southwest parallel to the continental coastline with the Sea of Japan in between. The land is located between approximately 20 to 45 degrees north latitude and between approximately 123 to 154 degrees east longitude. It consists of the main islands of Hokkaido, Honshu, Shikoku, Kyushu and Okinawa, and more than 6,800 smaller islands of various sizes. Its surface area totals 377,974 square kilometers.

Since the Japanese archipelago is located in the world's newest mobile belt, it is particularly prone to various geological phenomena. Therefore, the number of earthquakes in the country is quite high, and so is the proportion of active volcanoes. The land is full of undulations, with mountainous regions including hilly terrain accounting for about three-quarters of its total area. The mountains are generally steep and are intricately carved out by ravines. Hilly terrain extends between the mountainous regions and the plains.

Table 1.1
Surface Area of Japan (2022)

(Square kilometers)

District	Area
Japan	377,974
Honshu	231,234
Hokkaido	83,424
Kyushu	42,230
Shikoku	18,803
Okinawa	2,282

Source: Geospatial Information Authority of Japan.

Table 1.2
Top 10 Countries According to Surface Area (2020) [1]

(1,000 square kilometers)

Country	Area
World [2]	130,094
Russia	17,098
Canada	9,985
U.S.A.	9,834
China	9,600
Brazil	8,516
Australia	7,692
India	3,287
Argentina	2,796
Kazakhstan	2,725
Algeria	2,382

1) Comprising land area and inland waters. Excluding polar regions and uninhabited islands. 2) Land area only.
Source: United Nations.

2

Figure 1.1
Famous Mountains of the World

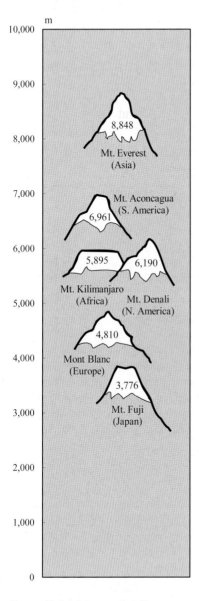

Source: National Astronomical Observatory of Japan.

Table 1.3
Mountains (As of February, 2022)

(Meters)

Name	Height
Mt. Fuji	3,776
Mt. Kitadake	3,193
Mt. Ainodake	3,190
Mt. Oku-Hotaka	3,190
Mt. Yarigatake	3,180
Mt. Higashidake	3,141
Mt. Akaishi	3,121
Mt. Karasawa	3,110
Mt. Kita-Hotaka	3,106
Mt. Obami	3,101

Source: Geospatial Information Authority of Japan.

Table 1.4
Rivers (As of April, 2021)

(Kilometers)

Name	Length
Shinano River	367
Tone River	322
Ishikari River	268
Teshio River	256
Kitakami River	249
Abukuma River	239
Kiso River	229
Mogami River	229
Tenryu River	213
Agano River	210

Source: Ministry of Land, Infrastructure, Transport and Tourism.

Table 1.5
Lakes (As of January, 2022)

(Square kilometers)

Name	Area
Lake Biwa	669.3
Lake Kasumigaura	168.2
Lake Saroma	151.6
Lake Inawashiro	103.2
Lake Nakaumi	85.7
Lake Kussharo	79.5
Lake Shinji	79.3
Lake Shikotsu	78.5
Lake Toya	70.7
Lake Hamana	64.9

Source: Geospatial Information Authority of Japan.

As of 2018, forestland and fields account for the largest portion of the nation's surface area. There are 25.38 million hectares of forestland and fields (which equates to 67.1 percent of the nation's surface area), followed by 4.42 million hectares of farmland (11.7 percent) combined. Together, forestland, fields and farmland thus cover approximately 80 percent of the nation. There are 1.96 million hectares of developed land (5.2 percent).

Table 1.6
Surface Area by Use

(million hectares)

Year	Total	Forestland and fields	Farmland	Inland water	Roads [1]	Developed land [2]	Others
1980	37.77	25.68	5.59	1.31	0.99	1.39	2.81
1990	37.77	25.52	5.33	1.31	1.14	1.60	2.87
2000	37.79	25.38	4.91	1.35	1.27	1.79	3.09
2010	37.79	25.35	4.67	1.33	1.36	1.90	3.19
2018	37.80	# 25.38	# 4.42	1.35	1.40	# 1.96	3.29
Percentage distribution (%)							
2018	100.0	67.1	11.7	3.6	3.7	5.2	8.7

1) Including farm roads and forest roads, etc. 2) Such as residential and industrial land.
Source: Ministry of Land, Infrastructure, Transport and Tourism.

2. Climate

Although the Japanese archipelago has a temperate marine climate, it differs by region depending on the effects of seasonal winds and ocean currents. Due to the topography of Honshu featuring a series of mountain ranges running from north to south, the northwest monsoon in the winter brings humid conditions with heavy precipitation (snow) to the Sea of Japan side of Honshu but comparatively dry weather with low precipitation to the Pacific Ocean side. In the summer, the southeast monsoon brings high temperatures and low rainfall on the Sea of Japan side, and high temperatures and high humidity on the Pacific Ocean side. Another unique characteristic of Japan's climate is that it has two long spells of rainy seasons, one in early summer when the southeast monsoon begins to blow, and the other in autumn when the winds cease. From summer to autumn, tropical cyclones generated in the Pacific Ocean to the south develop into typhoons and hit Japan, sometimes causing storm and flood damage. In recent years, intense torrential rains exceeding previous expectations have caused localized damage.

Figure 1.2
Temperature and Precipitation (Normal value)
(1991-2020 average)

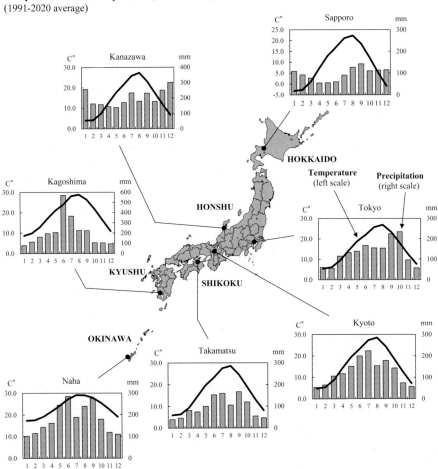

Source: Japan Meteorological Agency.

Table 1.7
Temperature and Precipitation (Normal value) (1991-2020 average)

Temperature (℃) Precipitation (mm)

Observing station			Jan.	Feb.	Mar.	Apr.	May	June	July	Aug.	Sep.	Oct.	Nov.	Dec.	Annual [1]
Sapporo	Temp.	High	-0.4	0.4	4.5	11.7	17.9	21.8	25.4	26.4	22.8	16.4	8.7	2.0	13.1
		Low	-6.4	-6.2	-2.4	3.4	9.0	13.4	17.9	19.1	14.8	8.0	1.6	-4.0	5.7
	Prec.		108	92	78	55	56	60	91	127	142	110	114	115	1,146
Tokyo	Temp.	High	9.8	10.9	14.2	19.4	23.6	26.1	29.9	31.3	27.5	22.0	16.7	12.0	20.3
		Low	1.2	2.1	5.0	9.8	14.6	18.5	22.4	23.5	20.3	14.8	8.8	3.8	12.1
	Prec.		60	57	116	134	140	168	156	155	225	235	96	58	1,598
Kanazawa	Temp.	High	7.1	7.8	11.6	17.3	22.3	25.6	29.5	31.3	27.2	21.8	15.9	10.2	19.0
		Low	1.2	1.0	3.4	8.2	13.6	18.4	22.9	24.1	19.9	13.9	8.1	3.5	11.5
	Prec.		256	163	157	144	138	170	233	179	232	177	251	301	2,402
Kyoto	Temp.	High	9.1	10.0	14.1	20.1	25.1	28.1	32.0	33.7	29.2	23.4	17.3	11.6	21.1
		Low	1.5	1.6	4.3	9.2	14.5	19.2	23.6	24.7	20.7	14.4	8.4	3.5	12.1
	Prec.		53	65	106	117	151	200	224	154	179	143	74	57	1,523
Takamatsu	Temp.	High	9.7	10.5	14.1	19.8	24.8	27.5	31.7	33.0	28.8	23.2	17.5	12.1	21.1
		Low	2.1	2.2	5.0	9.9	15.1	19.8	24.1	25.1	21.2	15.1	9.1	4.3	12.8
	Prec.		39	46	81	75	101	153	160	106	167	120	55	47	1,150
Kagoshima	Temp.	High	13.1	14.6	17.5	21.8	25.5	27.5	31.9	32.7	30.2	25.8	20.6	15.3	23.1
		Low	4.9	5.8	8.7	12.9	17.3	21.3	25.3	26.0	23.2	18.0	12.2	6.9	15.2
	Prec.		78	113	161	195	205	570	365	224	223	105	103	93	2,435
Naha	Temp.	High	19.8	20.2	21.9	24.3	27.0	29.8	31.9	31.8	30.6	28.1	25.0	21.5	26.0
		Low	14.9	15.1	16.7	19.1	22.1	25.2	27.0	26.8	25.8	23.5	20.4	16.8	21.1
	Prec.		102	115	143	161	245	284	188	240	275	179	119	110	2,161

1) Annual average for temperature and annual total for precipitation.
Source: Japan Meteorological Agency.

Chapter 2

Population

© Statistics Bureau, MIC

Okuizome is a traditional ceremony, celebrated 100 days after birth, where a baby pretends to eat his or her first meal.
There is a custom of placing pebbles on the festive table, in hopes the child will have sturdy teeth that are hard as rock.

1. Total Population

Japan's total population in 2021 was 125.50 million. This ranked 11th in the world and made up 1.6 percent of the world's total. Japan's population density measured 338.2 persons per square kilometer in 2020, ranking 12th among countries or areas with a population of 10 million or more.

Figure 2.1
Population Pyramid

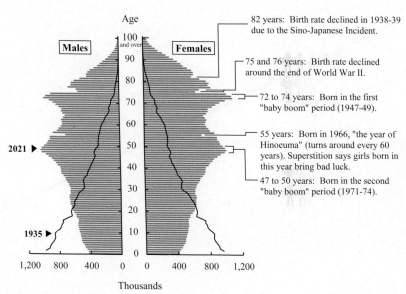

Source: Statistics Bureau, MIC.

Table 2.1
Countries with a Large Population (2021)

(Millions)

Country	Population	Country	Population
World	7,875	Brazil	214
China	1,444	Nigeria	211
India	1,393	Bangladesh	166
U.S.A.	333	Russia	146
Indonesia	276	Mexico	130
Pakistan	225	Japan	126

Source: Statistics Bureau, MIC; United Nations.

Figure 2.2
Population Density by Country or Area [1] **(2020)**

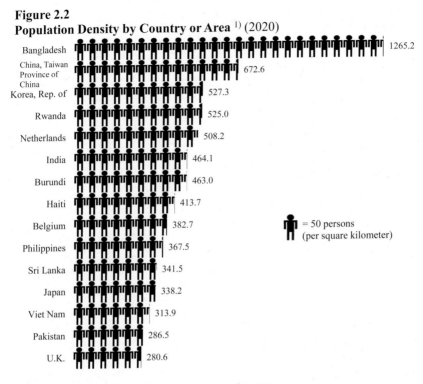

Country	Value
Bangladesh	1265.2
China, Taiwan Province of China	672.6
Korea, Rep. of	527.3
Rwanda	525.0
Netherlands	508.2
India	464.1
Burundi	463.0
Haiti	413.7
Belgium	382.7
Philippines	367.5
Sri Lanka	341.5
Japan	338.2
Viet Nam	313.9
Pakistan	286.5
U.K.	280.6

= 50 persons
(per square kilometer)

1) Top 15 countries or areas with a population of 10 million or more.
Source: Statistics Bureau, MIC; United Nations.

From the 18th century through the first half of the 19th century, Japan's population remained steady at about 30 million. Following the Meiji Restoration in 1868, it began expanding in tandem with the drive to build a modern nation-state. In 1912, it reached 50 million, and in 1967, it surpassed the 100 million mark. However, Japan's population growth slowed afterward, with the rate of population change about 1 percent from the 1960s through the 1970s. Since the 1980s, it has declined sharply. Japan's total population was 126.15 million according to the Population Census in 2020. The Population Census in 2015 marked the first decline in Japan's total population since the initiation of the Census in 1920. The decline continued in the Population Census in 2020, with a decrease of 948,646 people compared to the previous Census (2015). In 2021, it was 125.50 million, down by 0.64 million from the year before.

Table 2.2
Trends in Population (as of October 1)

Year	Population (1,000)	Age composition (%) [1]			Change rate of annual basis (%)	Population density (per km²)
		0-14 years old	15-64	65 years old and over		
1872 [2]	34,806	...	...	...	...	91
1900 [2]	43,847	33.9	60.7	5.4	0.83	115
1910 [2]	49,184	36.0	58.8	5.2	1.16	129
1920	55,963	36.5	58.3	5.3	1.30	147
1930	64,450	36.6	58.7	4.8	1.42	169
1940	71,933	36.7	58.5	4.8	1.10	188
1950	84,115	35.4	59.6	4.9	1.58	226
1955	90,077	33.4	61.2	5.3	1.38	242
1960	94,302	30.2	64.1	5.7	0.92	253
1965	99,209	25.7	68.0	6.3	1.02	267
1970	104,665	24.0	68.9	7.1	1.08	281
1975	111,940	24.3	67.7	7.9	1.35	300
1980	117,060	23.5	67.4	9.1	0.90	314
1985	121,049	21.5	68.2	10.3	0.67	325
1990	123,611	18.2	69.7	12.1	0.42	332
1995	125,570	16.0	69.5	14.6	0.31	337
2000	126,926	14.6	68.1	17.4	0.21	340
2005	127,768	13.8	66.1	20.2	0.13	343
2010	128,057	13.2	63.8	23.0	0.05	343
2015	127,095	12.6	60.9	26.6	-0.15	341
2020	126,146	11.9	59.5	28.6	-0.15	338
2021	125,502	11.8	59.4	28.9	-0.51	336
(Projection, 2017)						
2030	119,125	11.1	57.7	31.2	-0.58	319
2040	110,919	10.8	53.9	35.4	-0.71	297
2050	101,923	10.6	51.8	37.7	-0.84	273
2060	92,840	10.2	51.6	38.1	-0.93	249

1) The ratios for 2015 and 2020 were calculated using imputation values for unknowns. The ratios for 2010 and earlier were calculated by excluding unknowns from the denominator. 2) As of January 1.
Source: Statistics Bureau, MIC; National Institute of Population and Social Security Research; Geospatial Information Authority of Japan.

2. Households

(1) Household Size and Household Composition

The Population Census shows that Japan had 55.70 million private households (excluding "institutional households" such as students in school dormitories) in 2020. Of that total, 54.2 percent were nuclear-family households, and 38.1 percent were one-person households.

Figure 2.3
Changes in Household Composition

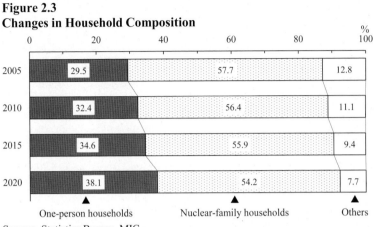

Source: Statistics Bureau, MIC.

From the 1920s to the mid-1950s, the average number of household members remained about 5. However, due to the increase in one-person households and nuclear-family households since the 1960s, the average size of households was down significantly in 1970, to 3.41 members. The number of household members has continued to decline, dropping to 2.21 in 2020. Although the Japanese population shifted into the declining phase, the number of households is expected to continue to increase for some years to come, as the size of the average household will shrink at a slow pace. The number of households is projected to peak in 2023 and then decrease thereafter.

Table 2.3

Households and Household Members [1]

Year	Private house-holds (1,000)	Rate of private households change (%) [2]	Private household members (1,000)	Members per household	Population (1,000)	Rate of population change (%) [2]
1960	22,539	...	93,419	4.14	94,302	4.7
1970	30,297	a) 15.9	103,351	3.41	104,665	5.5
1975	33,596	10.9	110,338	3.28	111,940	7.0
1980	35,824	6.6	115,451	3.22	117,060	4.6
1985	37,980	6.0	119,334	3.14	121,049	3.4
1990	40,670	7.1	121,545	2.99	123,611	2.1
1995	43,900	7.9	123,646	2.82	125,570	1.6
2000	46,782	6.6	124,725	2.67	126,926	1.1
2005	49,063	4.9	124,973	2.55	127,768	0.7
2010	51,842	5.7	125,546	2.42	128,057	0.2
2015	53,332	2.9	124,296	2.33	127,095	-0.8
2020	55,705	4.4	123,163	2.21	126,146	-0.7

1) In the 1965 Census, the definition of household differs, and it is not possible to recombine the survey subjects into private households.
2) Change over preceding Population Census.
a) The rate of change over 10 years is converted to a rate of change over 5 years.
Source: Statistics Bureau, MIC.

(2) Elderly Households

The number of elderly households (private households with household members aged 65 years old and over) in 2020 was 22.66 million. They accounted for 40.7 percent of the total private households. There were 6.72 million one-person elderly households. Among these, there were approximately two times as many females as males.

Table 2.4

Trends in Elderly Households

(Thousands)

Type of households	2005	2010	2015	2020
Private households	49,063	51,842	53,332	55,705
Elderly households	17,220	19,338	21,713	22,655
(percentage)	35.1	37.3	40.7	40.7
One-person households	3,865	4,791	5,928	6,717
Males	1,051	1,386	1,924	2,308
Females	2,814	3,405	4,003	4,409
Nuclear-family households	8,398	10,011	11,740	12,528
Others	4,956	4,536	4,045	3,410

Source: Statistics Bureau, MIC.

3. Declining Birth Rate and Aging Population

The population pyramid of 1950 shows that Japan had a standard-shaped pyramid with a broad base. The shape, however, has changed dramatically as both the birth rate and death rate have declined. In 2021, the aged population (65 years old and over) was 36.21 million, constituting 28.9 percent of the total population (i.e., 1 in every 4 persons) and marking a record high.

Figure 2.4
Changes in the Population Pyramid

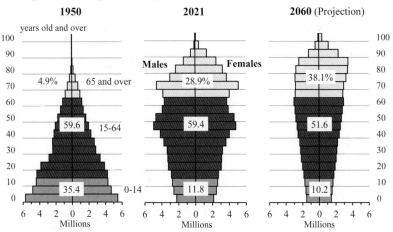

Source: Statistics Bureau, MIC;
National Institute of Population and Social Security Research.

In Japan, the percentage of persons aged 65 years old and over exceeded 10 percent in 1985, but as of 1950, this percentage was already 11.4 percent in France and 10.2 percent in Sweden. The percentage exceeded 10 percent in 1955 in Germany, 1965 in Italy, and 1970 in the U.S.A., all earlier than in Japan. However, in 2020, the percentage of the population aged 65 years old and over in Japan was 28.6 percent, exceeding the U.S.A. (16.6 percent), Sweden (20.3 percent), France (20.8 percent), Germany (21.7 percent), and Italy (23.3 percent), indicating that the aging society in Japan is progressing quite rapidly as compared to the U.S.A. and European countries.

Figure 2.5
Proportion of Elderly Population by Country (Aged 65 years old and over)

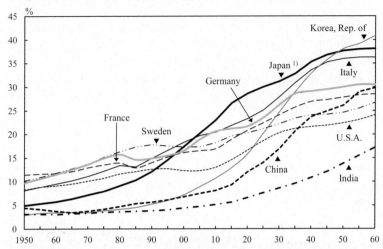

1) The ratios for 2015 and 2020 were calculated using imputation values for unknowns in the Population Census results. The ratios for 2010 and earlier were calculated by excluding unknowns from the denominator of Population Census results.

Source: Statistics Bureau, MIC; National Institute of Population and Social Security Research; United Nations.

Table 2.5
Age Structure of Population by Country

(%)

Country	2020			2060 (projection)		
	0-14 years old	15-64	65 years old and over	0-14 years old	15-64	65 years old and over
Korea, Rep. of	12.5	71.7	15.8	10.0	49.2	40.9
Japan [1]	11.9	59.5	28.6	10.2	51.6	38.1
Italy	13.0	63.7	23.3	11.4	52.3	36.3
Germany	14.0	64.4	21.7	14.2	55.3	30.5
China	17.7	70.3	12.0	14.0	56.2	29.8
France	17.7	61.6	20.8	15.3	56.3	28.5
Brazil	20.7	69.7	9.6	13.7	59.3	27.0
U.K.	17.7	63.7	18.7	15.4	57.6	27.0
Sweden	17.6	62.0	20.3	16.0	57.3	26.7
Canada	15.8	66.1	18.1	14.5	58.9	26.6
Russia	18.4	66.1	15.5	17.3	58.1	24.6
U.S.A.	18.4	65.0	16.6	16.2	59.7	24.1
India	26.2	67.3	6.6	17.1	65.8	17.2

1) The ratios for 2020 were calculated using imputation values for unknowns in the Population Census results.

Source: Statistics Bureau, MIC; National Institute of Population and Social Security Research; United Nations.

On the other hand, in 2021, the child population (0-14 years old) in Japan amounted to 14.78 million, accounting for 11.8 percent of the total population, which was the lowest level on record. Since 1997, the aged population (65 years old and over) have surpassed the child population in their proportion of the total population. The working age population (15-64 years old) totaled 74.50 million, accounting for 59.4 percent of the entire population. This population is continuing to decline since 1993. As a result, the dependency ratio (the sum of aged and child population divided by the working age population) was 68.5 percent.

4. Births and Deaths

Population growth in Japan had primarily been driven by natural increase, while social increase played only a minor part. However, in 2005, the natural change rate (per 1,000 population) became minus for the first time since 1899, and has been on a declining trend since then. In 2020, the natural change rate was -4.3 and decreased for the 14th consecutive year.

Figure 2.6
Natural Population Change

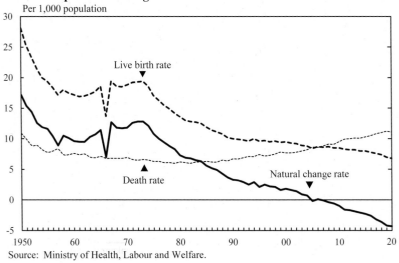

Source: Ministry of Health, Labour and Welfare.

During the second baby boom between 1971 and 1973, the live birth rate (per 1,000 population) was at a level of 19. Since the late 1970s, it has continued to fall. The rate for 2020 was 6.8. The decline in the live birth rate may partly be attributable to the rising maternal age at childbirth. The average mothers' age at first childbirth rose from 25.6 in 1970 to 30.7 in 2020.

The total fertility rate was on a downward trend after dipping below 2.00 in 1975, and reached a record low of 1.26 in 2005. The rate was on a path of recovery with an increase after that. However, the total fertility rate decreased for 5 consecutive years and dropped to 1.33 in 2020.

The death rate (per 1,000 population) was steady at 6.0 - 6.3 between 1975 and 1987, and has maintained an uptrend since 1988, reflecting the aging of the population. It reached 11.1 in 2020.

Table 2.6
Vital Statistics

Year	Rates per 1,000 population [1]				Total fertility rate [2]	Life expectancy at birth (years)	
	Live births	Deaths	Infant mortality	Natural change		Males	Females
1950	28.1	10.9	60.1	17.2	3.65	a) 59.57	a) 62.97
1955	19.4	7.8	39.8	11.6	2.37	63.60	67.75
1960	17.2	7.6	30.7	9.6	2.00	65.32	70.19
1965	18.6	7.1	18.5	11.4	2.14	67.74	72.92
1970	18.8	6.9	13.1	11.8	2.13	69.31	74.66
1975	17.1	6.3	10.0	10.8	1.91	71.73	76.89
1980	13.6	6.2	7.5	7.3	1.75	73.35	78.76
1985	11.9	6.3	5.5	5.6	1.76	74.78	80.48
1990	10.0	6.7	4.6	3.3	1.54	75.92	81.90
1995	9.6	7.4	4.3	2.1	1.42	76.38	82.85
2000	9.5	7.7	3.2	1.8	1.36	77.72	84.60
2005	8.4	8.6	2.8	-0.2	1.26	78.56	85.52
2010	8.5	9.5	2.3	-1.0	1.39	79.55	86.30
2015	8.0	10.3	1.9	-2.3	1.45	80.75	86.99
2020	6.8	11.1	1.8	-4.3	1.33	81.56	87.71

1) The infant mortality rate is per 1,000 live births.
2) The sum of the age-specific fertility rates from age 15 to 49 years old.
a) 1950-1952 period.
Source: Ministry of Health, Labour and Welfare.

Table 2.7
Changes of Mothers' Age at Childbirth

Year	Number of births (1,000) [1]	Distribution of mothers' age (%) [2]						Mean age bearing first child
		Under 19	20-24	25-29	30-34	35-39	40 and over	
1970	1,934	1.0	26.5	49.2	18.5	4.2	0.5	25.6
1980	1,577	0.9	18.8	51.4	24.7	3.7	0.5	26.4
1990	1,222	1.4	15.7	45.1	29.1	7.6	1.0	27.0
2000	1,191	1.7	13.6	39.5	33.3	10.6	1.3	28.0
2010	1,071	1.3	10.4	28.6	35.9	20.5	3.3	29.9
2015	1,006	1.2	8.4	26.1	36.3	22.7	5.4	30.7
2020	841	0.8	7.9	25.9	36.1	23.3	5.9	30.7

1) Including mothers' ages that were not reported. 2) Percentage in relation to number of births, excluding those for which mothers' ages were not reported.
Source: Ministry of Health, Labour and Welfare.

Average life expectancy in Japan climbed sharply after World War II, and is today at quite high level in the world. In 2020, it was 87.7 years for females and 81.6 years for males, setting a new all-time record for both genders.

Figure 2.7
Life Expectancy at Birth by Country

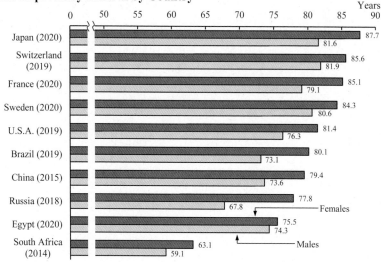

Source: Ministry of Health, Labour and Welfare.

17

5. Marriages and Divorces

It showed an apparent marriage boom in the early 1970s that the annual number of marriages in Japan exceeded 1 million couples coupled with the marriage rate (per 1,000 population) hovering over 10.0. However, both the number of couples and the marriage rate have been on a declining trend thereafter. In 2020, 525,507 couples married, and the marriage rate was 4.3.

The mean age of first marriage was 31.0 for grooms and 29.4 for brides in 2020. The mean age of first marriage for grooms rose by 2.2 years, while that of brides rose by 2.4 years over the past 20 years (in 2000: grooms, 28.8; brides, 27.0). In addition, there has been an increasing trend in the proportion of those who have never married until he or she turns the exact age 50, reaching 28.3 percent for males and 17.8 percent for females in 2020, the highest percentages ever. The declining marriage rate, rising marrying age and increased choice of unmarried life in recent years as described above could explain the dropping birth rate.

Table 2.8
Mean Age of First Marriage

Year	Grooms	Brides
1950	25.9	23.0
1955	26.6	23.8
1960	27.2	24.4
1965	27.2	24.5
1970	26.9	24.2
1975	27.0	24.7
1980	27.8	25.2
1985	28.2	25.5
1990	28.4	25.9
1995	28.5	26.3
2000	28.8	27.0
2005	29.8	28.0
2010	30.5	28.8
2015	31.1	29.4
2020	31.0	29.4

Source: Ministry of Health, Labour and Welfare.

Table 2.9
Proportion of Never Married at Exact Age 50 by Sex [1]

(%)

Year	Males	Females
1950	1.5	1.4
1960	1.3	1.9
1970	1.7	3.3
1980	2.6	4.5
1990	5.6	4.3
2000	12.6	5.8
2010	20.1	10.6
2015 [2]	24.8	14.9
2020 [2]	28.3	17.8

1) The proportion is computed as the mean value of the proportion remaining single at ages 45-49 and 50-54.
2) Based on results with imputation for persons of unknown marital status.
Source: National Institute of Population and Social Security Research.

In contrast, there was an upward trend about the divorces since the late 1960s, hitting a peak of 289,836 couples in 2002. Subsequently, both the number of divorces and the divorce rate have been declining since 2003. In 2020, the number of divorces totaled 193,253 couples, and the divorce rate (per 1,000 population) was 1.57.

Figure 2.8
Changes in Marriage Rate and Divorce Rate

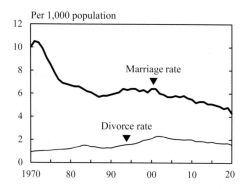

Source: Ministry of Health, Labour and Welfare.

6. Population Density and Regional Distribution

(1) Population Density

In 2020, Tokyo Metropolis had the largest population of 14.05 million among Japan's 47 prefectures, followed in decreasing order by the prefectures of Kanagawa, Osaka, Aichi, Saitama, Chiba, Hyogo, and Hokkaido. The top 8 prefectures in terms of population had a total population of 63.98 million, and accounted for more than 50 percent (50.7 percent) of the total population.

In addition, the population density in Tokyo Metropolis was the highest among Japan's prefectures, at 6,402.6 persons per square kilometer. This was almost 18.9 times larger than the national average (338.2 persons per square kilometer).

Figure 2.9
Population Density by Prefecture (2020)

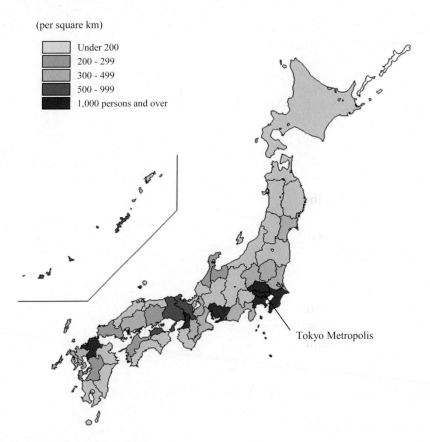

(per square km)

Under 200
200 - 299
300 - 499
500 - 999
1,000 persons and over

Tokyo Metropolis

Source: Statistics Bureau, MIC.

In 2020, there were 12 cities in Japan with a population of 1 million or more. Their total population topped 30 million, a figure equivalent to 24.0 percent of the national total. The largest single city was the 23 Cities of Tokyo Metropolis, with 9.73 million citizens. It was followed in decreasing order by Yokohama City (3.78 million), Osaka City (2.75 million), and Nagoya City (2.33 million).

Table 2.10
Population of Major Cities

(Thousands)

Cities	Population 2015	Population 2020	Cities	Population 2015	Population 2020
Tokyo, 23 Cities	9,273	9,733	Kawasaki City	1,475	1,538
Yokohama City	3,725	3,777	Kobe City	1,537	1,525
Osaka City	2,691	2,752	Kyoto City	1,475	1,464
Nagoya City	2,296	2,332	Saitama City	1,264	1,324
Sapporo City	1,952	1,973	Hiroshima City	1,194	1,201
Fukuoka City	1,539	1,612	Sendai City	1,082	1,097

Source: Statistics Bureau, MIC.

(2) Population Distribution

The percentage of the urban population started increasing in the late 1950s. In 2015, 51.9 percent of the total population was concentrated in the 3 major metropolitan areas: the Kanto, Chukyo, and Kinki major metropolitan areas. Population density in the Kanto major metropolitan area was 2,771 persons per square kilometer. In the Chukyo major metropolitan area, it was 1,288 persons per square kilometer, and in the Kinki major metropolitan area, it was 1,459 persons per square kilometer.

Table 2.11

Population of 3 Major Metropolitan Areas [1] (2015)

Areas	Population (1,000)	Percentage of the total (%)	Surface Area (km^2)	Population density (per km^2)
Kanto major metropolitan area	37,274	29.3	13,452	2,771
Chukyo major metropolitan area	9,363	7.4	7,271	1,288
Kinki major metropolitan area	19,303	15.2	13,228	1,459
Total of three major metropolitan areas	65,940	51.9	33,951	1,942

1) Major metropolitan areas consist of central cities (Kanto: 23 Cities of Tokyo Metropolis, Yokohama City, Kawasaki City, Sagamihara City, Saitama City, and Chiba City; Chukyo: Nagoya City; Kinki: Osaka City, Sakai City, Kyoto City, and Kobe City) and surrounding areas (cities, towns and villages).
Source: Statistics Bureau, MIC.

Chapter 3

Economy

© ITO Yoko

Contemplation. The Aichi Arts Center has museums, halls, galleries, and other facilities, offering a variety of performances and exhibitions enjoyed by men and women of all ages. When looking at Japan's net worth (national wealth), it was 3,668 trillion yen at the end of 2020.

1. Economic Development

During the 1960s, Japan's economy grew at a rapid pace of over 10 percent per annum. This rapid economic growth was supported by: (i) the expansion of private investments in plant and equipment, backed by a high rate of personal savings; (ii) a large shift in the working population from primary to secondary industries and "an abundant labour force supplied by a high rate of population growth"; and (iii) an increase in productivity brought about by adopting and improving foreign technologies.

Figure 3.1
Economic Growth Rates

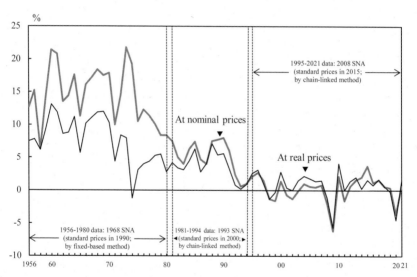

Source: Economic and Social Research Institute, Cabinet Office.

In the 1970s, the sharp increase of Japan's exports of industrial products to the U.S.A. and Europe began to cause international friction. In 1971, the U.S.A. announced it would end the convertibility of the dollar into gold. In December 1971, Japan revalued the yen from 360 yen against the U.S. dollar, which had been maintained for 22 years, to 308 yen. In February 1973, Japan adopted a floating exchange-rate system.

In October 1973, the fourth Middle East War led to the first oil crisis, triggering high inflation. Accordingly, Japan recorded negative economic growth in 1974 for the first time in the post-war period. Following the second oil crisis in 1978, efforts were made to change Japan's industrial structure from "energy-dependent" to "energy-saving", enabling Japan to successfully overcome inflation.

In the 1980s, the trade imbalance with advanced industrial countries expanded because of the yen's appreciation. As part of administrative and financial reforms, Japan National Railways and Nippon Telegraph and Telephone Public Corporation were privatized. As a result, domestic demand-led economic growth was achieved.

2. Bubble Economy and Its Collapse

At the end of the 1980s, Japan's economy enjoyed favorable conditions, with stable wholesale prices and a low unemployment rate. Corporate profits were at their highest level in history, and corporate failures were at their lowest level, while investments in plant and equipment for manufacturing products, such as semiconductors, were very active. Stock and land prices continued to rise rapidly, and large-scale urban developments and resort facility developments in rural areas progressed at a very fast pace. However, excessive funds flowed into the stock and real estate markets, causing abnormal increases in capital asset values (forming an economic bubble).

At the end of 1980, Japan's net worth (national wealth) stood at 1,363 trillion yen, 5.6 times the GDP. It then increased, reaching 3,531 trillion yen, 8.0 times the GDP, at the end of 1990, owing to increasing land and stock prices. At the beginning of 1990, stock prices plummeted, followed by sharp declines in land prices. This marked the start of major economic recession (collapse of the bubble economy). Japan's financial and economic systems, which were excessively dependent on land, consequently approached collapse.

Due to the collapse of the bubble economy, the national wealth decreased, and while there were fluctuations, continued on a downward trend. Since 2012, it has been on an upward trend. At the end of 2020, it was 3,668 trillion yen.

Figure 3.2
National Wealth [1]

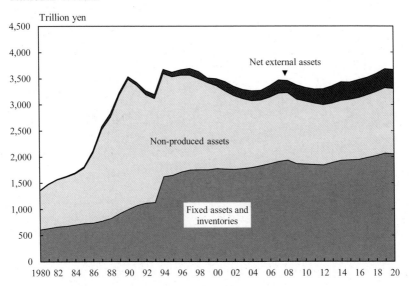

Trillion yen

1) Data was estimated using a different method beginning in 1994.
Source: Economic and Social Research Institute, Cabinet Office.

Massive bad debts were created in financial institutions' loan portfolios, as corporate borrowers suffered serious losses due to declining land prices. As a result, shareholders' equity in financial institutions shrank. In 1997, large banks began to fail. In 1998 and 1999, the government injected public money into the banking sector to stabilize the financial system.

The Japanese economy began to make a moderate recovery in February 1999. This, however, was only a temporary phenomenon, as investments in plant and equipment were weak and the recovery was too dependent on foreign demand and information and communication technologies. With the global decline in IT demand from mid-2000, Japan's exports to Asia dropped, necessitating adjustments of excess inventory and production facilities. In line with this, the Japanese economy again entered into an economic downturn in 2001.

Figure 3.3
Gross Domestic Product (Nominal prices, converted into U.S. dollars)

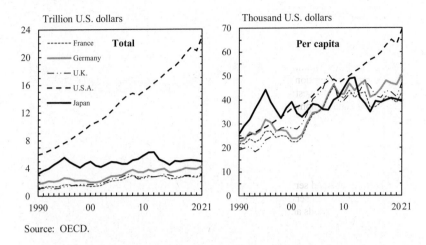

Source: OECD.

On the economic recovery phase starting at the beginning of 2002, the corporate sector, with export-related industries, as the central part, became favorable based on the steady recovery of the global economy, and shifted generally with a bullish tone up until mid-2007.

3. Recent Economic Trends

At the start of 2008, the Japanese economy was faced with a standstill in its path to recovery as private consumption and investments in plant and equipment fell flat and so did production. This occurred against the backdrop of soaring crude petroleum and raw material prices and repercussions from the American subprime mortgage loan problem that, since mid-2007, rapidly clouded future prospects for the world economy further. In addition, the bankruptcy of the major American securities firm Lehman Brothers in September 2008 led to a serious financial crisis in Europe and the U.S.A. Japan was also affected by the yen's rise and the sudden economic contraction in the U.S.A. and other countries. Declining exports contributed to a large drop in production and a sharp rise in unemployment.

Table 3.1

Gross Domestic Product [1] (Expenditure approach)

(Billion yen)

Item	2018	2019	2020	2021
Gross domestic product (GDP)	554,439.5	553,106.9	528,230.7	536,792.4
Domestic demand	551,690.5	552,837.3	532,363.8	535,691.6
Private demand	415,719.8	414,393.3	390,234.0	392,311.3
Private final consumption expenditure	302,635.0	300,998.0	285,206.3	288,995.1
Private Residential Investment	19,834.5	20,645.7	19,016.0	18,663.5
Private plant and equipment	91,203.7	91,297.7	85,388.6	84,793.9
Changes in inventories of private sectors	2,101.7	1,487.0	650.9	-146.9
Public demand	135,971.9	138,445.0	142,128.0	143,380.1
Government final consumption expenditure	108,431.2	110,503.0	113,041.9	115,422.4
Gross capital formation by public sectors	27,572.9	28,029.6	29,125.6	28,059.9
Changes in inventories of public sectors	-11.2	-57.0	-24.1	-28.5
Net exports of goods and services	2,875.6	323.6	-4,491.3	1,211.4
Exports of goods and services	105,465.2	103,927.0	91,666.4	102,336.1
(less) Imports of goods and services	102,589.6	103,603.5	96,157.7	101,124.7
(Reference)				
Trading gains/losses	-2,727.8	-2,033.6	2,992.4	-4,052.1
Gross domestic income (GDI)	551,711.8	551,073.4	531,223.1	532,740.3
Net income from the rest of the world	21,171.5	21,610.3	19,308.8	20,262.6
Incomes from the rest of the world	33,156.1	33,966.9	29,558.1	30,806.5
(less) Incomes to the rest of the world	11,984.6	12,356.6	10,249.3	10,543.9
Gross national income (GNI)	572,883.2	572,683.7	550,532.0	553,002.9

1) Quarterly estimates of GDP, 2008 SNA (standard prices in 2015; by chain-linked method).
Source: Economic and Social Research Institute, Cabinet Office.

Subsequently, the Japanese economy recovered with foreign demand and economic measures after April 2009, and came to a standstill starting around October 2010. In early 2011, however, it began to rally. The Great East Japan Earthquake taking place on March 11, 2011, and the nuclear power plant accident caused by it weakened the economic recovery.

In order to achieve an early end to deflation and break free of economic stagnation, in January 2013, the government set forth its "three-arrows" strategy (also known as "Abenomics").

The first "arrow" is "aggressive monetary policy". The Bank of Japan (BOJ) made it clear that it would set two percent annual growth rate of consumer price index as a "price stabilization target". The BOJ also introduced "quantitative and qualitative monetary easing" to double the monetary base over two years.

The second "arrow" is "flexible fiscal policy". An emergency economic stimulus package with a scale of approximately 10 trillion yen was developed.

The third "arrow" is "growth strategy that promotes private investment". Efforts are being made in growth strategies such as encouraging investments by private corporations based on the easing of regulations.

Figure 3.4
Economic Growth Rates [1] (Quarterly changes)

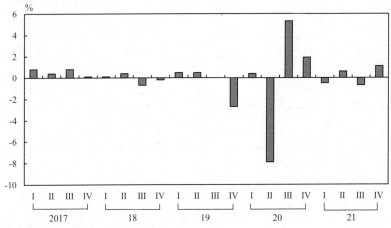

1) Quarterly estimates of GDP, 2008 SNA (standard prices in 2015; by chain-linked method; seasonally adjusted).
Source: Economic and Social Research Institute, Cabinet Office.

Amidst these initiatives, the Japanese economy has continued to show signs of moderate recovery, with profits of companies at high levels. However, due to factors like the slowdown in the Chinese economy, and a lull in global demand for information-related goods, weakness has been evident in some areas of export and production since the second half of 2018. On the other hand, the increasing trend in domestic demand has been maintained, supported by factors like improvement in the employment and income environment, and high company profits. In the year 2020, Japan's economy was hit by an unprecedented economic slowdown due to the global COVID-19 pandemic. In 2021, economic activities in Japan were intermittently restrained to prevent the spread of infection. Although the economy was in the recovery phase, the pace was slow.

4. Industrial Structure

Japan's industrial structure has undergone a major transformation since the end of World War II. The chronological changes in the industrial structure during this period by industry share of employed persons and GDP show that shares in the primary industry in particular have fallen dramatically since 1970, when Japan experienced rapid economic growth. During the 1980s, the secondary industry's share of employed persons and GDP also began to decline gradually. On the other hand, the tertiary industry's share of them have risen consistently.

Table 3.2
Changes in Industrial Structure

(%)

Year	Employed persons [1)2)]			Gross domestic product (GDP) [3)]		
	Primary industry	Secondary industry	Tertiary industry	Primary industry	Secondary industry	Tertiary industry
1950	48.6	21.8	29.7	...	...	...
1955	41.2	23.4	35.5	19.2	33.7	47.0
1960	32.7	29.1	38.2	12.8	40.8	46.4
1965	24.7	31.5	43.7	9.5	40.1	50.3
1970	19.3	34.1	46.6	5.9	43.1	50.9
1975	13.9	34.2	52.0	5.3	38.8	55.9
1980	10.9	33.6	55.4	# 3.5	# 36.2	# 60.3
1985	9.3	33.2	57.5	3.0	34.9	62.0
1990	7.2	33.5	59.4	2.4	35.4	62.2
1995	# 6.0	# 31.3	# 62.7	# 1.7	# 31.5	# 66.9
2000	5.2	29.5	65.3	1.5	29.2	69.3
2005	4.9	26.4	68.6	1.1	26.8	72.1
2010	4.2	25.2	70.6	1.1	25.5	73.4
2015	3.7	24.6	71.7	1.0	25.9	73.1
2020	3.2	23.4	73.4	1.0	25.9	73.1

1) Due to the revision of the Japan Standard Industrial Classification, the figures from 1995 onward are not strictly consistent with those for 1990 or earlier. 2) Ratios for 2015 and 2020 use imputation values for unknowns. 3) The data for 1955 to 1975 are based on the 1968 SNA, the data for 1980 to 1990 are based on the 1993 SNA, and the data for 1995 onwards are based on the 2008 SNA.
Source: Statistics Bureau, MIC; Economic and Social Research Institute, Cabinet Office.

In 1970, the primary industry accounted for 19.3 percent of employed persons, the secondary industry for 34.1 percent, and the tertiary industry for 46.6 percent. In 2020, the corresponding shares of these three sectors were 3.2 percent, 23.4 percent and 73.4 percent, respectively.

As for GDP by type of economic activity, in 1970, the primary, secondary and tertiary industries accounted for 5.9 percent, 43.1 percent and 50.9 percent, respectively. In 2020, these figures were 1.0 percent, 25.9 percent and 73.1 percent, respectively.

Table 3.3

Gross Domestic Product by Type of Economic Activity

(%)

	1995	2000	2005	2010	2015	2020
Primary industry						
Agriculture, forestry and fishing	1.6	1.5	1.1	1.1	1.0	1.0
Secondary industry						
Mining	0.2	0.1	0.1	0.1	0.1	0.1
Manufacturing	23.5	22.5	21.4	20.8	20.5	19.7
Construction	7.6	6.7	5.4	4.6	5.2	5.9
Tertiary industry						
Electricity, gas and water supply and waste management service	3.1	3.3	3.0	2.9	2.9	3.3
Wholesale and retail trade	13.8	13.0	14.1	13.4	13.0	12.6
Transport and postal services	5.5	4.9	5.1	5.1	5.3	4.3
Accommodation and food service activities	3.0	3.1	2.7	2.6	2.4	1.8
Information and communications	3.3	4.7	5.0	5.0	4.9	5.1
Finance and insurance	5.1	5.0	6.1	4.8	4.3	4.3
Real estate	10.3	10.8	11.0	12.3	12.0	12.2
Professional, scientific and technical activities	4.5	5.5	6.2	7.2	7.8	8.4
Public administration	4.7	5.0	5.0	5.1	4.9	5.2
Education	3.6	3.6	3.6	3.7	3.5	3.6
Human health and social work activities	4.2	5.1	5.7	6.7	7.4	8.2
Other service activities	5.2	5.2	4.9	4.6	4.2	3.7

Source: Economic and Social Research Institute, Cabinet Office.

According to the "2016 Economic Census for Business Activity", there were 5.3 million establishments (excluding businesses whose operational details are unknown, national government services, and local government services) in Japan, at which a total of 56.9 million persons were employed. The average number of persons engaged per establishment was 10.6 and establishments with less than 10 persons accounted for 77.3 percent of the total.

Figure 3.5

Shares of Establishments and Persons Engaged by Scale of Operation [1)]
(2016)

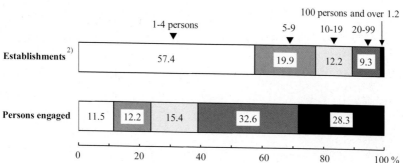

1) Excluding businesses whose operational details are unknown, national government services, and local government services. 2) Excluding establishments consisting of only loaned or dispatched employees.
Source: Statistics Bureau, MIC; Ministry of Economy, Trade and Industry.

With regard to the number of establishments by the major groupings of the Japan Standard Industrial Classification, the most numerous category was the "wholesale and retail trade", numbering 1.4 million, followed by "accommodations, eating and drinking services" and "construction". In terms of the number of persons engaged, establishments in the "wholesale and retail trade" ranked first as they employed 11.8 million persons, followed by "manufacturing" and "medical, health care and welfare".

Table 3.4
Number of Establishments and Persons Engaged [1] (2016)

Item	Establishments	Persons engaged
Total	5,340,783	56,872,826
By industry		
Primary industry		
Agriculture, forestry and fisheries	32,676	363,024
Secondary industry		
Mining and quarrying of stone and gravel	1,851	19,467
Construction	492,734	3,690,740
Manufacturing	454,800	8,864,253
Tertiary industry		
Electricity, gas, heat supply and water	4,654	187,818
Information and communications	63,574	1,642,042
Transport and postal activities	130,459	3,197,231
Wholesale and retail trade	1,355,060	11,843,869
Finance and insurance	84,041	1,530,002
Real estate and goods rental and leasing	353,155	1,462,395
Scientific research, professional and technical services	223,439	1,842,795
Accommodations, eating and drinking services	696,396	5,362,088
Living-related and personal services and amusement services	470,713	2,420,557
Education, learning support	167,662	1,827,596
Medical, health care and welfare	429,173	7,374,844
Compound services	33,780	484,260
Services, n.e.c.	346,616	4,759,845
By type of legal organizations		
Individual proprietorships	2,006,773	5,719,403
Corporations	3,305,188	51,032,017
Companies	2,882,491	42,716,541
Organizations other than corporations	28,822	121,406

1) Excluding businesses whose operational details are unknown, national government services, and local government services.
Source: Statistics Bureau, MIC; Ministry of Economy, Trade and Industry.

The domestic manufacturing industry has progressed in the relocation of production bases overseas, for the cutback on production costs, the production in consumption areas, and the evasion of fluctuations in exchange rates.

The number of overseas affiliates in the manufacturing industry was 11,070 companies at the end of fiscal 2020, and the overseas production ratio was 23.6 percent in actual performance in fiscal 2020.

Table 3.5

Trends of Overseas Affiliated Company (Manufacturing industries)

Fiscal year	Number of overseas affiliates [1]	Value of Sales (Million yen)	Overseas production ratio [2] (%)	Value of capital investment (Million yen)	Ratio of overseas capital investment [3] (%)
2011	8,684	88,289,996	18.0	3,082,273	21.5
2012	10,425	98,384,657	20.3	3,815,707	25.8
2013	10,545	116,997,649	22.9	4,646,055	29.4
2014	10,592	129,712,997	24.3	4,649,364	28.1
2015	11,080	134,996,164	25.3	4,571,639	25.5
2016	10,919	123,636,074	23.8	3,766,446	20.7
2017	10,838	138,024,661	25.4	3,961,088	20.8
2018	11,344	138,584,467	25.1	4,384,020	21.5
2019	11,199	121,618,532	23.4	4,292,606	22.1
2020	11,070	112,790,400	23.6	3,219,364	19.4

1) End of fiscal year. 2) Overseas production ratio = Sales of overseas affiliates/(Sales of overseas affiliates + Sales of domestic companies) × 100.

3) Ratio of overseas capital investment = Amount of capital investment in overseas affiliates/(Amount of capital investment in overseas affiliates + Amount of capital investment in domestic companies) × 100.

Source: Ministry of Economy, Trade and Industry.

In the future, it is anticipated that companies in the manufacturing industry in Japan will expand their overseas business. There are many companies that are planning on expanding their business to China, India, the U.S.A., and Vietnam.

Chapter 4

Finance

© IIDA Masahide

Nightscapes Marunouchi. Marunouchi is the name of a district in Chiyoda City, Tokyo. It is located east of the Imperial Palace. This district is home to Tokyo Station, and a center of finance and economy in Japan, with a concentration of the headquarters and offices of banks and companies.

1. National and Local Government Finance

(1) National Government Finance

Japan's fiscal year starts in April, and ends in March of the following year. In setting the national budget, the government submits a proposed budget for the upcoming fiscal year to the Ordinary Session of the Diet, which begins in January. The proposal is then discussed, and approved usually before the fiscal year begins in April (initial budget). In the event that the Diet does not approve the budget by the end of March, an interim budget comes into effect. The interim budget is effective from the beginning of April until such time when the proposed budget is approved. If it becomes necessary to amend the budget in the course of a fiscal year, the government submits a supplementary budget for Diet approval. As with the fiscal 2021 supplementary budget, the initial budget for fiscal 2022 also includes a contingency fund for COVID-19.

Japan's national budget consists of the general account budget, special account budgets, and the budgets of government-affiliated agencies. Using revenues from general sources such as taxes, the general account covers core national expenditures such as social security, public works, education and science, and national defense.

Special accounts are accounts established for the national government to carry out projects with specific objectives, and their management and administration are independent of the general account. The number and particulars of special accounts change from year to year; for fiscal 2022, there are a total of 13 special accounts, including the National debt consolidation fund, the Local allocation tax and local transfer tax, and the Reconstruction from the Great East Japan Earthquake.

Government-affiliated agencies are entities established by special laws and are entirely funded by the government. Currently, the Japan Finance Corporation, the Okinawa Development Finance Corporation, Japan Bank for International Cooperation, and the Japan International Cooperation Agency (Finance and Investment Account) are operated.

Figure 4.1
Revenue and Expenditure in the General Account [1]

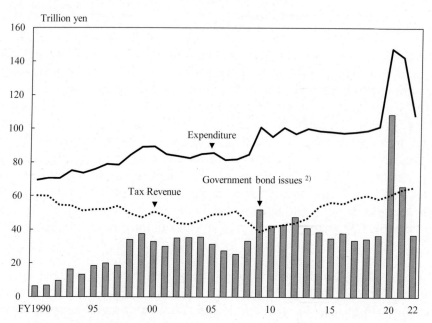

Trillion yen

1) Based on settled figures until FY2020, supplementary budget for FY2021, and draft budget for FY2022. 2) Excludes some special accounts.
Source: Ministry of Finance.

In the national government finance, expenditure has continued to surpass revenue. Since fiscal 2008 in particular, the worsening economy has decreased tax revenue, contributing to an increasing gap between revenue and expenditure. From fiscal 2009 to fiscal 2012, bond issues exceeded tax revenue in most years, but starting in fiscal 2013, tax revenue began to exceed borrowing. However, in fiscal 2020, the supplementary budget for the contingency fund for COVID-19 was covered solely by government bonds, leading to bond issues exceeding tax revenue.

The size of the general account budget for fiscal 2022 was 108 trillion yen, an increase of 1.0 trillion yen (0.9 percent) from the initial budget of fiscal 2021. This is equivalent to 19.1 percent of the fiscal 2022 GDP, forecasted by the government at 565 trillion yen.

Table 4.1
Expenditures of General Account

(Billion yen)

Fiscal year	Total (A)+(B)+(C)	General expenditures (A)	Social security	Education and science	Pensions	National defense	Public works
2000	89,321	52,046	17,636	6,872	1,418	4,907	11,910
2005	85,520	49,343	20,603	5,701	1,065	4,878	8,391
2010	95,312	56,978	28,249	6,051	709	4,670	5,803
2015	98,230	58,966	31,398	5,574	387	5,130	6,378
2019	101,366	63,048	33,501	5,911	202	5,627	7,610
2020	147,597	109,016	42,998	9,194	169	5,505	8,413
2021 [1]	142,599	98,337	46,942	8,110	145	6,080	8,052
2022 [2]	107,596	67,375	36,274	5,390	122	5,369	6,058

Fiscal year	Economic cooperation	Small and medium-sized business promotion	Energy measures	Food stable supply	Others	National debt service (B)	Local allocation tax grants, etc. (C)
2000	1,012	933	677	247	6,434	21,446	15,829
2005	784	237	493	657	6,536	18,736	17,441
2010	746	830	845	1,122	7,953	19,544	18,790
2015	661	340	968	1,276	6,854	22,464	16,801
2019	653	779	1,049	1,121	6,596	22,286	16,032
2020	763	16,257	1,027	1,498	23,190	22,326	16,256
2021 [1]	669	4,145	1,266	1,770	21,157	24,705	19,558
2022 [2]	511	171	876	1,270	11,335	24,339	15,883

1) Revised budget. 2) Initial budget.
Source: Ministry of Finance.

In fiscal 2022, major expenditures from the initial general account budget include social security (33.7 percent), national debt service (22.6 percent), local allocation tax grants, etc. (14.8 percent), public works (5.6 percent), education and science (5.0 percent), and national defense (5.0 percent).

With regard to revenue sources for the fiscal 2022 initial general account budget, consumption tax, income tax and corporation tax account for 51.3 percent. Even with the addition of other taxes and stamp revenues, these revenue sources only amount to 60.6 percent of the total revenue.

Figure 4.2
Composition of Revenue and Expenditure of General Account Budget
(Initial budget, FY2022)

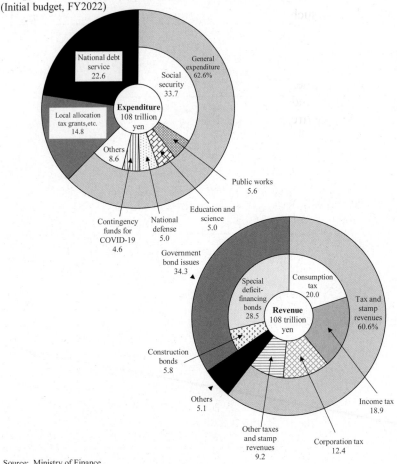

Source: Ministry of Finance.

(2) Local Government Finance

There are two budget categories in local government finance: the ordinary accounts and the public business accounts. The former covers all kinds of expenses related to ordinary activities of the prefectural and municipal governments. The latter covers the budgets of independently accounted enterprises such as public enterprises (water supply and sewerage systems, hospitals, etc.), the national health insurance accounts, and the latter-stage elderly medical care accounts.

While expenditures such as defense expenses are administered solely by the national government, a large portion of expenditures that directly relate to the people's daily lives are disbursed chiefly through local governments. In particular, a high proportion of the following expenditures are disbursed through local governments: sanitation expenses, which include areas such as medical service and garbage disposal; school education expenses; judicial, police, and fire service expenses; and public welfare expenses, which cover the development and management of welfare facilities for children, the elderly, and the mentally and/or physically challenged.

The revenue composition of local governments usually remains almost the same each fiscal year, while their budget scale and structure vary from year to year. The largest portion of fiscal 2020 (net) revenues came from local taxes, accounting for 31.4 percent of the total. The second-largest source, 28.8 percent, was national treasury disbursements.

Table 4.2

Local Government Finance [1] (Ordinary accounts)

(Million yen)

Item	FY2016	FY2017	FY2018	FY2019	FY2020
Revenues	101,459,848	101,323,315	101,345,285	103,245,881	130,047,239
Local taxes	39,392,391	39,904,402	40,751,442	41,211,450	40,825,620
Local transfer tax	2,340,232	2,405,224	2,650,873	2,613,842	2,232,335
Special local grants	123,300	132,800	154,400	468,271	225,609
Local allocation tax	17,239,008	16,768,005	16,548,225	16,739,246	16,988,952
National treasury disbursements	15,687,149	15,520,357	14,885,189	15,834,380	37,455,724
Local bonds	10,387,277	10,644,892	10,508,424	10,870,548	12,260,718
Expenditures	98,141,464	97,998,369	98,020,611	99,702,189	125,458,842
General administration	8,901,591	9,121,944	9,285,987	9,670,029	22,534,636
Public welfare	26,340,756	25,983,397	25,665,947	26,533,656	28,694,223
Sanitation	6,258,413	6,262,562	6,236,691	6,353,956	9,120,199
Agriculture, forestry and fishery	3,171,208	3,299,187	3,251,691	3,319,243	3,410,589
Commerce and industry	5,195,146	4,901,049	4,760,301	4,782,097	11,533,589
Civil engineering work	12,018,244	11,919,457	11,880,636	12,127,421	12,690,157
Education	16,745,847	16,888,597	16,878,150	17,523,493	18,096,094

1) Settled figures of the net total of prefectural and municipal government accounts after deducting duplications. The breakdown consists of major items only.

Source: Ministry of Internal Affairs and Communications.

(3) National and Local Government Finance

Finance refers to revenue and expenditure of administrative services from national and local governments. In the initial budget for fiscal 2021, the gross total of national government expenditure was 604 trillion yen, the net total was 299 trillion yen after eliminating duplications between both accounts. Furthermore, the local public finance plan, which consists of the estimated sum of ordinary accounts for the following fiscal year for all local governments, amounted to 90 trillion yen. Therefore, after eliminating duplications between national and local accounts (35 trillion yen), the net total of both national and local government expenditures combined was 354 trillion yen.

Table 4.3
Expenditures of National and Local Governments (Initial budget)

(Billion yen)

Item	FY2000	FY2005	FY2010	FY2015	FY2020	FY2021
General account	84,987	82,183	92,299	96,342	102,658	106,610
Special accounts	318,689	411,944	367,074	403,553	391,759	493,699
Government-affiliated agencies	7,661	4,678	3,135	2,216	1,722	3,234
Gross total (national)	411,337	498,805	462,508	502,111	496,139	603,542
Duplications	200,435	257,490	244,744	262,184	250,273	304,750
Net total (national)	210,902	241,316	217,764	239,927	245,867	298,792
Local public finance plan	88,930	83,769	82,127	87,768	91,747	90,248
Gross total (national + local)	299,832	325,084	299,891	327,694	337,614	389,040
Duplications	37,216	32,689	31,563	35,484	36,241	35,390
Net total (national + local)	262,616	292,395	268,328	292,211	301,373	353,650

Source: Policy Research Institute, Ministry of Finance.

The settlement amount for fiscal 2020, the net total of national and local government expenditures was 223 trillion yen. The national government disbursed 44.0 percent of this amount, while the local governments disbursed 56.0 percent.

Figure 4.3
Ratio of Net Total National and Local Expenditures by Function

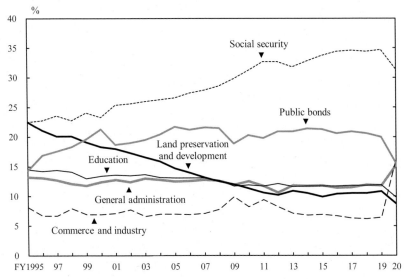

Source: Ministry of Internal Affairs and Communications.

A function-by-function breakdown of these expenditures showed that social security expenditure accounted for the largest portion (31.4 percent), followed by commerce and industry (16.2 percent), public bonds (15.5 percent), general administration (15.2 percent), education (9.8 percent), and then land preservation and development (8.7 percent). Public bonds are issued to compensate for shortages of national and local revenues. Their issue volumes have increased mainly due to, for example, economic stimulus measures and decreasing tax revenues after the bubble economy ended at the beginning of 1990. The bankruptcy of the major American securities firm Lehman Brothers in 2008 and the Great East Japan Earthquake of 2011 led to a major economic downturn, and for 4 years from fiscal 2009, bond issues continued to exceed tax revenue, but from fiscal 2013 to 2019, tax revenue picked up and exceeded bond issues. However, the spread of COVID-19 in 2020 caused a sudden contraction of the economy, and a huge supplementary budget for fiscal 2020 was financed by an additional issue of government bonds.

Figure 4.4
National Government Bond Issue and Bond Dependency Ratio [1]

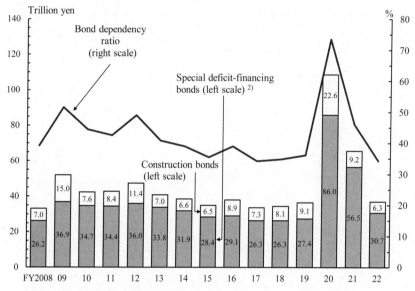

1) Based on settled figures until FY2020, supplementary budget for FY2021, and draft budget for FY2022. 2) Excludes some special accounts.
Source: Ministry of Finance.

Japan's ratio of outstanding general government debt to GDP, a stock measure in a fiscal context, is particularly high even compared to other major industrialized countries.

Figure 4.5
Ratio of General Government Gross Debt to GDP

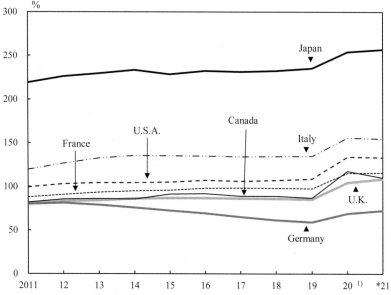

1) The data for Japan indicates estimated figure.
Source: Ministry of Finance.

(4) Tax

Taxes consist of national tax (income tax, corporation tax, etc.), which is paid to the national government, and local tax, which is paid to the local government of the place of payer's residence. The ratio of taxation burden, which is the ratio of national and local taxes to national income, was 18.3 percent in fiscal 1975. This ratio gradually increased thereafter, reaching 27.7 percent in fiscal 1989. The ratio subsequently decreased due to the decline in tax revenue arising from the recession that ensued after the bubble economy ended, reaching 20.5 percent in fiscal 2003. In fiscal 2019, it was 25.8 percent in terms of national and local taxes combined (15.5 percent for national tax and 10.3 percent for local tax). Japan's ratio is lower in comparison with other major industrial countries. However, the consumption tax rate was raised from 8 to 10 percent on October 1, 2019 due to the need to transition Japan's social security system, which is currently focused on benefits for the elderly, to an "all-generation type" usable by anyone, from children and youth to the elderly.

Figure 4.6
Ratio of Taxation Burden to National Income by Country (Actual basis)

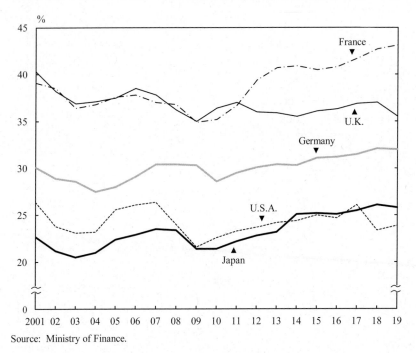

Source: Ministry of Finance.

2. Bank of Japan and Money Stock

As the central bank, the Bank of Japan (i) issues banknotes; (ii) manages and stores treasury funds and provides loans to the government; (iii) provides deposit and loan services to general financial institutions; and (iv) implements monetary policies by adjusting the level of money stock to promote the sound development of the economy.

At the end of 2021, currency in circulation totaled 127.0 trillion yen (122.0 trillion yen in banknotes and 5.1 trillion yen in coins), up 3.0 percent from the year before.

Table 4.4

Currency in Circulation (Outstanding at year-end)

(Billion yen)

Item	2017	2018	2019	2020	2021
Total	111,508	115,208	117,695	123,381	127,026
Banknotes	106,717	110,363	112,742	118,328	121,964
Coins	4,792	4,845	4,954	5,053	5,062

Source: Bank of Japan.

The Bank of Japan compiles and publishes statistics on the following indices of money stock: (i) M1, or currency in circulation plus deposit money deposited at depository institutions; (ii) M2, or currency in circulation plus deposits deposited at domestically licensed banks, etc.; (iii) M3, or currency in circulation plus deposits deposited at depository institutions; and (iv) L, or M3 plus pecuniary trusts plus investment trusts plus bank debentures plus straight bonds issued by banks plus commercial paper issued by financial institutions plus government securities plus foreign bonds. The average amounts outstanding of money stock in 2021 was 969 trillion yen in M1 and 1,163 trillion yen in M2.

Table 4.5

Money Stock [1] (Average amounts outstanding)

(Billion yen)

Year	M2	M3	M1	Quasi-money	CDs	L (Broadly-defined liquidity)
2017	973,993	1,299,628	711,885	556,268	31,475	1,735,482
2018	1,002,456	1,332,502	755,601	546,672	30,229	1,772,981
2019	1,026,203	1,359,458	795,675	534,908	28,875	1,802,499
2020	1,092,630	1,432,440	882,257	521,668	28,515	1,875,877
2021	1,162,696	1,511,685	968,978	508,400	34,307	1,981,095

1) "Money stock" indicates the aggregate amount of money, including currency in circulation and deposit money, held by money holders such as non-financial corporations, individuals, and local governments.

Source: Bank of Japan.

In January 2013, the government and the Bank of Japan decided to strengthen policy coordination in order to overcome deflation and achieve sustainable economic growth with stable prices. In April 2013, the Bank of Japan changed the operating target for money market operations from the uncollateralized overnight call rate to a monetary base to facilitate quantitative easing. The Bank of Japan first introduced Quantitative and Qualitative Monetary Easing (QQE) in April 2013; in January 2016, it decided to introduce "QQE with a Negative Interest Rate". In September 2016, it was decided to introduce "QQE with Yield Curve Control" by strengthening these two policy frameworks, in order to achieve as early as possible the "price stability target" of a 2 percent year-on-year increase in consumer prices. In April 2020, the Bank of Japan decided to further intensify monetary easing in response to the economic downturn caused by COVID-19.

Japan's monetary base is the amount of currency supplied by the Bank of Japan. It is the combined total of banknotes in circulation, coins in circulation, and current account deposit in the Bank of Japan. It was 688.4 trillion yen as of the end of April 2022, up 5.0 percent from the same month of the previous year, and setting a new record high.

Table 4.6
Financial Markets (Interest rates, etc.)

(% per annum)

End of year	Basic discount rate and basic loan rate	Call rates [1]	Prime lending rates [2]	Average contract interest rates on loans and discounts [3]	10 years' newly issued Govt. bond yields
2012	0.30	0.076	1.475	1.034	0.795
2013	0.30	0.068	1.475	0.880	0.740
2014	0.30	0.066	1.475	0.850	0.320
2015	0.30	0.038	1.475	0.778	0.265
2016	0.30	-0.058	1.475	0.623	0.040
2017	0.30	-0.062	1.475	0.584	0.045
2018	0.30	-0.055	1.475	0.597	-0.005
2019	0.30	-0.068	1.475	0.602	-0.025
2020	0.30	-0.033	1.475	0.481	0.020
2021	0.30	-0.018	1.475	0.475	0.070

1) Uncollateralized overnight. 2) Principal banks. Short-term loans.
3) Outstanding loans and bills discounted. Short-term loans and discounts. Figures are those of banking accounts of domestically licensed banks (excluding several banks) that conduct transactions with the Bank of Japan.
Source: Bank of Japan.

3. Financial Institutions

In addition to the Bank of Japan, Japan's financial system is comprised of private and public financial institutions. Private financial institutions include those that accept deposits (banks, credit depositories, agricultural cooperatives, etc.) and those that do not (securities companies, insurance companies, etc.).

In the course of the financial system reform, mergers and restructuring progressed among major banks, resulting in their being reorganized into three major financial groups. The number of regional banks and credit depositories has also declined significantly due to the progress of corporate mergers. As of the end of September 2021, in the number of offices operated domestically, including the branches of financial institutions, post offices had the largest network with 23,794 offices. Domestically licensed banks, including city banks and regional banks, had a combined total of 13,543 offices and branches.

The fundamental role of the bank sector is to adjust the surplus and deficiency of funds. The corporate sector has been in a fund surplus throughout the 2021 year, and thus the percentage of loans to bank assets has generally been on a consistent downward trend.

Figure 4.7
Assets of Domestically Licensed Banks (Banking accounts, end of year)

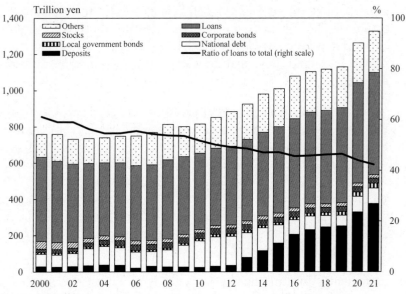

Source: Bank of Japan.

4. Financial Assets

The Flow of Funds Accounts Statistics, which is a comprehensive set of records of financial transactions, assets and liabilities, indicates that financial assets in the domestic sectors totaled 8,764 trillion yen at the end of March 2021. Of these assets, those of the domestic nonfinancial sector were 4,025 trillion yen. Of this sector, the household sector (including the business funds of individual proprietorships) had assets of 1,968 trillion yen, in the forms of deposits, stocks and other financial assets. In Japan, the household sector holds more than 50 percent of its financial assets in cash and deposits.

Table 4.7
Financial Assets and Liabilities of Japan

(Billion yen)

Sectors	March 2020	March 2021	Annual change (%)
Financial assets			
Domestic sectors	7,882,295	8,763,610	11.2
Financial institutions	4,250,940	4,738,843	11.5
Domestic nonfinancial sector	3,631,355	4,024,767	10.8
Nonfinancial corporations	1,142,937	1,287,430	12.6
General government	614,321	706,204	15.0
Households (incl. individual proprietorships)	1,816,597	1,967,973	8.3
Private nonprofit institutions serving households ..	57,500	63,160	9.8
Overseas	735,963	825,566	12.2
Financial liabilities			
Domestic sectors	7,519,122	8,386,999	11.5
Financial institutions	4,108,892	4,559,040	11.0
Domestic nonfinancial sector	3,410,230	3,827,959	12.2
Nonfinancial corporations	1,701,973	2,033,225	19.5
General government	1,324,089	1,401,831	5.9
Households (incl. individual proprietorships)	354,142	361,526	2.1
Private nonprofit institutions serving households ..	30,027	31,378	4.5
Overseas	1,094,845	1,197,084	9.3

Source: Bank of Japan.

5. Stock Market

Stock prices in Japan rose sharply in the second half of the 1980s, spearheading the bubble economy. However, it started to fall in 1990 ahead of land prices. At the end of 1989, the total market capitalization in the Tokyo Stock Exchange First Section was 591 trillion yen, but only 3 years later, it had dropped by more than 50 percent to 281 trillion yen. Even after recovering to 442 trillion yen at the end of 1999, the stock market repeatedly fell and rose afterwards. The bankruptcy of the major American securities firm Lehman Brothers in September 2008 led to a fall in total market capitalization, which amounted to 251 trillion yen at the end of 2011. From 2012 to 2021, there has been major upturn as a result of the effects of various measures, including a comprehensive economic policy package called "Abenomics".

Figure 4.8
Stock Price Index and Market Capitalization
(Tokyo Stock Exchange First Section, end of year)

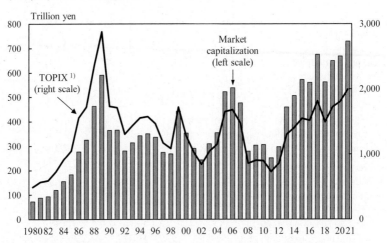

1) A free-float adjusted market capitalization-weighted index that is calculated based on all the domestic common stocks listed on the Tokyo Stock Exchange First Section. It shows the measure of current market capitalization assuming that market capitalization as of the base date (January 4 ,1968) is 100 points.
Source: Tokyo Stock Exchange, Inc.

In 2012, the high yen in Japanese economy was corrected due to expectations toward anti-deflationary economic and fiscal policies by the new government, and share prices soared. In April 2013, changes in policies of the Bank of Japan were regarded as affecting stocks and markets, and the Nikkei Stock Average at the end of 2013 was 16,291.31 yen, representing an increase of 56.7 percent as compared to that of the end of 2012 (10,395.18 yen) and the first significant gain in 8 years. Afterwards, the Nikkei Stock Average in April 2015 recovered to the 20,000 yen level for the first time in 15 years. The closing value at the end of 2021 was 28,791.71 yen, up 1,347.54 yen, or 4.9 percent for the year, exceeding the previous year for the third consecutive year.

Table 4.8

Stock Prices (Tokyo Stock Exchange First Section)

Year	Number of listed companies [1]	Market capitalization [1] (million yen)	Total trading value (million yen)	TOPIX [1][2] Tokyo stock price index, average	Nikkei Stock Average (225 issues) [1] (yen)
2000	1,447	352,784,685	242,632,346	1,283.67	13,785.69
2001	1,491	290,668,537	199,844,292	1,032.14	10,542.62
2002	1,495	242,939,136	190,869,955	843.29	8,578.95
2003	1,533	309,290,031	237,905,753	1,043.69	10,676.64
2004	1,595	353,558,256	323,918,214	1,149.63	11,488.76
2005	1,667	522,068,129	459,136,406	1,649.76	16,111.43
2006	1,715	538,629,548	644,308,788	1,681.07	17,225.83
2007	1,727	475,629,039	735,333,528	1,475.68	15,307.78
2008	1,715	278,988,813	568,538,950	859.24	8,859.56
2009	1,684	302,712,168	368,679,737	907.59	10,546.44
2010	1,670	305,693,030	354,598,763	898.80	10,228.92
2011	1,672	251,395,748	341,587,524	728.61	8,455.35
2012	1,695	296,442,945	306,702,280	859.80	10,395.18
2013	1,774	458,484,253	640,193,836	1,302.29	16,291.31
2014	1,858	505,897,342	576,525,070	1,407.51	17,450.77
2015	1,934	571,832,889	696,509,496	1,547.30	19,033.71
2016	2,002	560,246,997	643,205,780	1,518.61	19,114.37
2017	2,062	674,199,186	683,218,254	1,817.56	22,764.94
2018	2,128	562,121,332	740,746,041	1,494.09	20,014.77
2019	2,160	648,224,522	598,213,662	1,721.36	23,656.62
2020	2,186	666,862,093	671,671,658	1,804.68	27,444.17
2021	2,182	728,424,514	765,249,832	1,992.33	28,791.71
2022 Jan.	2,183	692,139,369	64,238,692	1,895.93	27,001.98
Feb.	2,178	688,618,750	62,740,408	1,886.93	26,526.82
Mar.	2,175	708,523,421	81,350,111	1,946.40	27,821.43
Apr.	# 1,837	# 683,684,685	# 24,354,567	1,899.62	26,847.90

1) End of year or month. 2) A free-float adjusted market capitalization-weighted index that is calculated based on all the domestic common stocks listed on the Tokyo Stock Exchange First Section. It shows the measure of current market capitalization assuming that market capitalization as of the base date (January 4 ,1968) is 100 points.

Source: Tokyo Stock Exchange, Inc.; Nikkei Inc.

At the end of March 2021, the total number of individual stockholders (individuals of Japanese nationality and domestic groups without corporate status) in possession of stocks listed on the Tokyo/Nagoya/Fukuoka/ Sapporo Stock Exchanges totaled 59.8 million. In terms of value, the ratio of stocks they possessed was 16.8 percent, up 0.3 percentage points from the previous fiscal year. The ratio of Japanese stocks held by foreign investors (total of corporations and individuals) was 30.2 percent in terms of value, up 0.6 percentage points from the previous fiscal year.

A survey conducted by the Japan Securities Dealers Association (JSDA) showed that 33.1 percent of 266 securities firms offered Internet trading at the end of September 2021. Internet trading thus accounted for 24.5 percent of the total value of stock brokerage transactions from April to September 2021.

Chapter 5

Agriculture, Forestry, and Fisheries

Set-net fishing. A fishing technique where, starting at high tide in the early morning, triangular jib nets (about 3 meters x 2 meters) are sunk under the water to catch small fish that swim in with the tide.

1. Overview of Agriculture, Forestry, and Fisheries

Over the course of Japan's economic growth, its agricultural, forestry and fishing industries have employed fewer and fewer workers every year, and their nominal GDP share has also dropped. The number of employed persons decreased from 5.77 million in 1980 (10.4 percent of the total employed persons) to 2.13 million in 2020 (3.2 percent), and the GDP share of the industries fell from 3.6 percent in 1980 to 1.0 percent in 2020.

Figure 5.1
Number of Employed Persons [1] **and**
Percentage of Gross Domestic Product (Nominal prices) [2] **for**
Agriculture, Forestry, and Fisheries

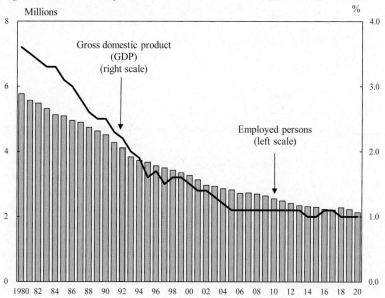

1) 1980-2001 data: The 10th revision of the Japan Standard Industrial Classification (JSIC). 2002-2020 data: The 12th and 13th revisions of JSIC. 2) 1980-1993 data: 1993 SNA, Benchmark year = 2000. 1994-2020 data: 2008 SNA, Benchmark year = 2015.
Source: Statistics Bureau, MIC; Economic and Social Research Institute, Cabinet Office.

2. Agriculture

(1) Agricultural Production

Japan's total agricultural output in 2020 was 8.94 trillion yen, up 0.5 percent from the previous year. Among this, crops yielded 5.66 trillion yen, up 0.5 percent from the previous year. Livestock yielded 3.24 trillion yen, up 0.8 percent from the previous year.

Table 5.1
Total Agricultural Output

(Billion yen)

Item	2016	2017	2018	2019	2020
Total	9,203	9,274	9,056	8,894	8,937
Crops	5,980	5,961	5,782	5,630	5,656
Rice	1,655	1,736	1,742	1,743	1,643
Vegetables	2,557	2,451	2,321	2,152	2,252
Fruits and nuts	833	845	841	840	874
Livestock and its products	3,163	3,252	3,213	3,211	3,237
Beef cattle	739	731	762	788	739
Dairy cattle	870	896	911	919	925
Pigs	612	649	606	606	662
Chickens	875	903	861	823	833

Source: Ministry of Agriculture, Forestry and Fisheries.

Table 5.2
Agricultural Harvest

(Thousand tons)

Products	2016	2017	2018	2019	2020
Cereal grains					
Rice	8,044	7,824	7,782	7,764	7,765
Wheat	791	907	765	1,037	949
Vegetables, sweet potatoes, and beans					
Potatoes	2,199	2,395	2,260	· 2,399	2,205
Sweet potatoes	861	807	797	749	688
Soybeans	238	253	211	218	219
Cucumbers	550	560	550	548	539
Tomatoes	743	737	724	721	706
Cabbages	1,446	1,428	1,467	1,472	1,434
Chinese cabbages	889	881	890	875	892
Onions	1,243	1,228	1,155	1,334	1,357
Lettuces	586	583	586	578	564
Japanese radishes	1,362	1,325	1,328	1,300	1,254
Carrots	567	597	575	595	586
Fruits					
Mandarins	805	741	774	747	766
Apples	765	735	756	702	763
Grapes	179	176	175	173	163
Japanese pears	247	245	232	210	171
Industrial crops					
Crude tea [1]	80	82	86	82	70
Sugar beets [2]	3,189	3,901	3,611	3,986	3,912

1) Production. 2) Area of Hokkaido prefecture.
Source: Ministry of Agriculture, Forestry and Fisheries.

(2) Agriculture Management Entity and Cultivated Land

In 2020, there were 1.076 million agriculture management entities (entities producing agricultural products, or performing contract agricultural work, where the area or number of animals involved in the production or work is as stipulated), a decrease of around 302,000 entities (21.9 percent) compared to 2015.

Among agriculture management entities, there were 1.037 million individual management entities (non-corporate family management entities), a decrease of around 303,000 entities (22.6 percent) compared to 2015. Group management entities (entities other than individual management entities) increased by around 1,000 entities (2.8 percent) to around 38,000 entities.

Table 5.3
Number of Agriculture Management Entities

(Thousand entities)

Year	Agriculture management entities	Individual management entities	Group management entities	Corporated management entities
2010	1,679	1,644	36	22
2015	1,377	1,340	37	27
2020	1,076	1,037	38	31
Percent change (%)				
2015 / 2010	-18.0	-18.5	4.9	25.3
2020 / 2015	-21.9	-22.6	2.8	13.3

Source: Ministry of Agriculture, Forestry and Fisheries.

Average agriculture gross income for all farming types and all agriculture management entities (individual management entities and corporated management entities) in 2020 was 9.92 million yen, an increase of 7.2 percent compared to the previous year. On the other hand, agriculture expenditures increased 7.7 percent compared to the previous year to 8.69 million yen. As a result, agriculture income increased by 3.8 percent compared to the previous year to 1.23 million yen.

Japan's cultivated acreage shrank year after year from 6.09 million hectares in 1961 to 4.35 million hectares in 2021. After 1989, the cultivated acreage has continued to decrease due to diversion into residential land, ruined land continuously resulting from devastated land, etc.

3. Forestry

As of 2017, Japan's forest land area is 25.05 million hectares (approximately 70 percent of the entire surface area of the country). Among Japan's forests, natural forests account for 13.48 million hectares, while planted forests, most of which are conifer plantations, make up 10.20 million hectares.

Japan's forest growing stock is 5,242 million cubic meters as of 2017, 3,308 million cubic meters of which are from planted forests. The stock rose mainly with the increase of that from planted forests on deforested sites right after World War II and during the period of rapid economic growth. Such forests are in a period of full-scale use as resources. There is a need to further promote use of domestic timber as lumber in housing, public buildings, etc., and as biomass, for reasons such as effective use of forest resources, proper management and manifestation of the diverse functions of forests, development of the forestry industry and mountainous areas, and mitigation of global warming.

Table 5.4
Forest Land Area and Forest Resources (2017)

Item	Total	National forest	Non-national forest		
			Public	Private	Others
Forest land area (1,000 ha)	25,048	7,659	2,995	14,347	48
Forest growing stock (million m³) ..	5,242	1,226	616	3,394	6
Planted forest					
Land area (1,000 ha)	10,204	2,288	1,334	6,569	13
Growing stock (million m³)	3,308	513	397	2,396	3
Natural forest					
Land area (1,000 ha)	13,481	4,733	1,531	7,188	28
Growing stock (million m³)	1,932	712	218	999	3

Source: Ministry of Agriculture, Forestry and Fisheries.

After reaching a low of 16.9 million cubic meters in 2002, domestic wood supply is on a rising trend, against the background of an enrichment of forest resources, increase in the use of domestic timber such as Japanese cedar for plywood material, increase in use of domestic timber in wood biomass power generation facilities, etc.

Figure 5.2
Wood Supply and Self-Sufficiency Rate [1)]

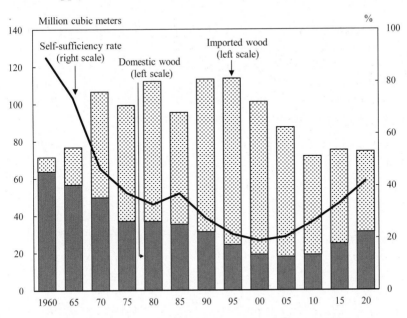

1) Wood supply refers to the sum of wood for industrial use, fuel wood and wood for mushroom production converted into a log equivalent.
Source: Ministry of Agriculture, Forestry and Fisheries.

Securing a forestry labor force will be vital not only for forestry, but also for creating employment based on local resources, and revitalizing mountain villages by promoting permanent residence. The number of workers engaged in forestry occupations such as stand tending and tree felling is in a declining trend over the long term, and decreased by around 7,000 workers from around 52,000 in 2005 to around 45,000 in 2015.

4. Fisheries

(1) Fishery Production

Japan is facing a problem in that its fishery production is in a declining trend over the long term. This is likely due to a variety of factors, such as changes in the marine environment and more intensive operations by foreign fishing boats in waters surrounding Japan. There are thought to be many fishery resources whose decline could have been prevented or mitigated with more appropriate resource management.

After peaking in 1984, Japan's fishery output decreased rapidly until around 1995, and has continued to decrease gradually afterwards. Its 2021 fishery production totaled 4.17 million tons.

Figure 5.3
Production by Type of Fishery

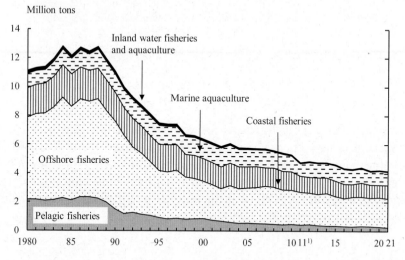

1) Excluding figures lost in Iwate, Miyagi and Fukushima prefectures because of the Great East Japan Earthquake.
Source: Ministry of Agriculture, Forestry and Fisheries.

Table 5.5

Production by Fishery Type and Major Kinds of Fish

(Thousand tons)

Fishery type and species	2017	2018	2019	2020	2021[*]
Total	4,306	4,421	4,197	4,234	4,173
Marine fishery	3,258	3,360	3,229	3,213	3,191
Tunas	169	165	161	177	142
Skipjack, Frigate mackerel	227	260	237	196	231
Sardine	500	522	556	698	682
Mackerels	518	542	450	390	434
Shellfishes	284	350	386	382	389
Crabs	26	24	23	21	21
Squids	103	84	73	82	62
Marine aquaculture	986	1,005	915	970	931
Yellowtails	139	138	136	138	133
Oysters	174	177	162	159	158
Laver ("nori")	304	284	251	289	244
Seaweed ("wakame")	51	51	45	54	44
Pearl (tons)	20	21	19	16	13
Inland water fishery	25	27	#22	22	18
Salmons, trouts	6	8	#7	7	5
Sweet fish	2	2	#2	2	2
Shellfishes	13	13	#10	9	9
Inland water aquaculture	37	30	31	29	33
Eel	21	15	17	17	21
Trouts	8	7	7	6	6
Sweet fish	5	4	4	4	4

Source: Ministry of Agriculture, Forestry and Fisheries.

(2) Fishery Workers

The number of fishery workers (those aged 15 years old and over who have worked at sea for 30 days or more in the past year) continues to decline. In 2020, the number of such workers was 135,660 workers, down 6.3 percent.

Table 5.6

**Enterprises and Workers Engaged in the Marine Fishery/
Aquaculture Industry**

Year	Enterprises			Workers		
	Total	Individual households	Corporate entities	Total	Self-employed	Hired
2005	126,020	118,930	7,090	222,170	...	...
2010	103,740	98,300	5,440	202,880	128,270	74,610
2015	85,210	80,570	4,640	166,610	100,520	66,100
2019	73,270	68,900	4,370	144,740	80,290	64,450
2020	69,560	65,310	4,250	135,660	75,810	59,850

Source: Ministry of Agriculture, Forestry and Fisheries.

While the aging of workers and fishing vessels progresses fisheries have been gaining attention as a place for employment, based on the diversification of values regarding work and life, and support is being provided for new fishery workers.

5. Self-Sufficiency in Food

Japan's food self-sufficiency ratio in terms of calories has shown a downward trend over the long term. It fell to 40 percent in fiscal 1998, and has fluctuated roughly around that level since. Whereas the ratio was 53 percent in fiscal 1985, it was 37 percent in fiscal 2020. The major reason behind the decrease in the food self-sufficiency ratio is that while declining in consumption of rice, for which demand can be met with domestic production, diversification of the Japanese dietary life has led to increased consumption of livestock products and oils and fats, for which overseas dependence for feed and raw materials is inevitable.

In fiscal 2020, the self-sufficiency ratio per item (on weight basis) was 97 percent for rice, 15 percent for wheat, 8 percent for beans, 80 percent for vegetables, 38 percent for fruits, 53 percent for meat, and 55 percent for seafood. While almost completely self-sufficient in rice, the staple food of its people, Japan rely almost entirely on imports for the supply of wheat and beans.

Table 5.7

Domestic Production, Supplies for Domestic Consumption,
Food Self-Sufficiency Ratio, and Imports

Fiscal year	Domestic production (1,000 t)	Supplies for domestic consumption (1,000 t)	Food self-sufficiency Ratio (%)	Imports (1,000 t)
Rice				
2000	9,490	9,790	95	879
2005	8,998	9,222	95	978
2010	8,554	9,018	97	831
2015	8,429	8,600	98	834
2020*	8,145	7,857	97	814
Wheat				
2000	688	6,311	11	5,688
2005	875	6,213	14	5,292
2010	571	6,384	9	5,473
2015	1,004	6,583	15	5,660
2020*	949	6,412	15	5,521
Beans				
2000	366	5,425	7	5,165
2005	352	4,790	7	4,482
2010	317	4,035	8	3,748
2015	346	3,789	9	3,511
2020*	290	3,843	8	3,411
Vegetables				
2000	13,704	16,826	81	3,124
2005	12,492	15,849	79	3,367
2010	11,730	14,508	81	2,783
2015	11,856	14,776	80	2,941
2020*	11,474	14,361	80	2,946
Fruits				
2000	3,847	8,691	44	4,843
2005	3,703	9,036	41	5,437
2010	2,960	7,719	38	4,756
2015	2,969	7,263	41	4,351
2020*	2,685	7,110	38	4,490
Meat				
2000	2,982	5,683	52	2,755
2005	3,045	5,649	54	2,703
2010	3,215	5,769	56	2,588
2015	3,268	6,035	54	2,769
2020*	3,452	6,540	53	3,043
Seafood				
2000	5,736	10,812	53	5,883
2005	5,152	10,201	51	5,782
2010	4,782	8,701	55	4,841
2015	4,194	7,663	55	4,263
2020*	3,714	6,794	55	3,885

Source: Ministry of Agriculture, Forestry and Fisheries.

Japan's present food self-sufficiency ratio is the lowest among major industrialized countries, and Japan is thus the world's leading net importer of agricultural products.

Figure 5.4
Trends in Food Self-Sufficiency Ratio of Major Countries [1)]
(On calorie supply basis)

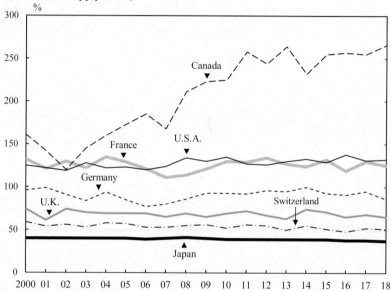

1) Estimates except for Japan.
Source: Ministry of Agriculture, Forestry and Fisheries.

Chapter 6

Manufacturing and Construction

© SHIBASAKI Shizuo

A pontoon bridge in the Seto region. Sea fog of the strait near the Kurushima Bridge. The "Seto Ohashi Bridge" traverses the Seto Inland Sea, linking Honshu and Shikoku. It consists of three suspension bridges, two cable-stayed bridges, and one truss bridge, and the name "Seto Ohashi Bridge" is used to refer collectively to these six long-span bridges, and the viaducts which connect them. This is one of the world's largest dual purpose bridges for both automobiles and trains. (The top part is a highway while the lower part is a railway.)

1. Overview of the Manufacturing Sector

The proportion of added value produced in Japan's manufacturing sector to its nominal GDP has been around 20 percent recently, and the sector has a large ripple effect on other sectors.

In years past, Japan's manufacturing industry has faced a variety of unforeseeable circumstances and drastic changes in the business environment. These include the Nixon Shock and two oil crises in the 1970s, the strong yen recession following the Plaza Accord in the 1980s, the bursting of the bubble economy and the Asian currency crisis in the 1990s, and the bankruptcy of the major American securities firm Lehman Brothers, the European debt crisis, and the Great East Japan Earthquake in the 21st century. Each time that Japan's manufacturing industry has faced these kinds of unforeseeable circumstances and drastic changes in the business environment, it has been able to overcome them and evolve. However, to overcome the recent crisis caused by COVID-19 will require even more substantial reforms than before.

In 2020, there were 181,877 establishments (with 4 or more persons engaged) in the manufacturing sector. By industry, "fabricated metal products" had the most, with 25,094 establishments (component ratio of 13.8 percent), followed by "food" with 23,648 establishments (13.0 percent) and "production machinery" with 18,273 establishments (10.0 percent).

In 2020, there were 7.72 million persons engaged, and by industry, "food" had the most, with 1.14 million persons engaged (component ratio of 14.7 percent), followed by "transportation equipment" with 1.06 million persons engaged (13.8 percent) and "production machinery" with 0.62 million persons engaged (8.1 percent).

The value of manufactured goods shipments in 2019 was 322.53 trillion yen, and by industry, "transportation equipment" had the most at 67.99 trillion yen (component ratio of 21.1 percent), followed by "food" at 29.86 trillion yen (9.3 percent) and "chemical and allied products" at 29.25 trillion yen (9.1 percent).

Table 6.1

Establishments, Persons Engaged, and Value of Manufactured Goods Shipments of the Manufacturing Industry [1]

Industries	Number of establish-ments (2020)	Number of persons engaged (2020)	Value of manu-factured goods shipments (2019) (billion yen)
Manufacturing	181,877	7,717,646	322,533
Food	23,648	1,136,951	29,857
Beverages, tobacco and feed	3,898	103,462	9,602
Textile products	10,586	239,139	3,694
Lumber and wood products [2]	4,613	87,554	2,811
Furniture and fixtures	4,578	89,287	1,986
Pulp, paper and paper products	5,338	187,842	7,688
Printing and allied industries	9,661	251,733	4,845
Chemical and allied products	4,650	381,259	29,253
Petroleum and coal products	915	27,000	13,844
Plastic products [3]	12,119	451,650	12,963
Rubber products	2,256	117,393	3,336
Leather tanning, leather products and fur skins	1,057	19,483	326
Ceramic, stone and clay products	9,024	237,550	7,653
Iron and steel	4,015	223,524	17,748
Non-ferrous metals and products	2,475	140,206	9,614
Fabricated metal products	25,094	612,427	15,965
General-purpose machinery	6,615	327,541	12,162
Production machinery	18,273	622,006	20,853
Business oriented machinery	3,727	211,175	6,753
Electronic parts, devices and electronic circuits	3,789	410,504	14,124
Electrical machinery, equipment and supplies	8,306	502,824	18,229
Information and communication electronics equipment	1,183	122,202	6,712
Transportation equipment	9,538	1,064,560	67,994
Miscellaneous manufacturing industries	6,519	150,374	4,521

1) Establishments with 4 or more persons engaged. 2) Excluding furniture.
3) Excluding plastic furniture, plastic plate making for printing, etc., which are included in other industrial classification.
Source: Ministry of Economy, Trade and Industry.

With regard to the "Indices on Mining and Manufacturing" (2015 average=100), the production index for 2021 was 95.7, up 5.6 percent from the previous year, while shipments stood at 93.7, an increase of 4.6 percent from the year before.

Table 6.2

Indices on Mining and Manufacturing (2021)

(2015 average =100)

Industries	Production [1]	Annual growth (%)	Shipments	Annual growth (%)	Inventory [2]	Annual growth (%)	Inventory Ratio [3]	Annual growth (%)
Mining and manufacturing	95.7	5.6	93.7	4.6	97.8	4.9	112.2	-10.1
Manufacturing	95.7	5.5	93.7	4.6	97.8	4.9	112.2	-10.1
Iron, steel and non-ferrous metals	94.1	13.0	94.0	10.5	104.2	16.4	107.7	-12.7
Iron and steel	92.7	15.7	92.0	13.7	103.9	17.4	109.7	-13.8
Fabricated metals	90.0	4.0	89.9	2.4	86.2	-3.6	105.1	-9.5
Production machinery	115.9	21.6	116.8	21.0	87.6	13.6	96.1	-19.0
General-purpose and business oriented machinery	99.8	10.9	98.2	11.3	126.8	10.0	144.7	-10.8
General-purpose machinery	100.7	12.1	102.3	13.4	123.3	16.0	110.8	-12.1
Electronic parts and devices	110.4	14.5	102.8	12.7	72.2	25.3	70.5	-21.2
Electrical machinery, and information and communication electronics equipment	94.2	6.2	95.7	6.8	95.6	6.1	124.5	-4.6
Electrical machinery	100.3	7.7	100.6	8.4	105.5	8.1	126.5	-4.5
Information and communication electronics equipment	79.1	1.7	83.2	2.2	58.8	-5.9	118.2	-5.3
Transport equipment	85.8	-0.8	86.4	-0.9	80.4	-5.2	96.2	-5.5
Ceramics, stone and clay products	93.1	3.9	93.8	4.0	96.5	3.3	112.7	-7.0
Chemicals	99.7	3.5	98.2	2.8	107.1	-1.8	111.6	-16.6
Petroleum and coal products	78.7	0.3	79.7	-1.0	90.8	3.1	116.3	-1.2
Plastic products	100.6	3.1	100.7	2.5	110.7	5.8	109.4	-1.7
Pulp, paper and paper products	91.4	3.0	88.6	2.3	94.5	2.7	115.4	-10.1
Foods and tobacco	96.9	-0.7	94.3	-1.4	96.0	2.8	144.4	-0.6
Other manufacturing	85.4	4.8	85.4	3.9	96.8	-1.9	110.1	-10.9
Mining	86.6	-0.7	96.0	3.3	105.4	-8.8	125.5	-8.7
(Reference) Electricity, gas, heat supply and water	98.6	1.8	98.8	1.6	-	-	-	-

1) Value added weights. 2) End of the year. 3) Inventory ratio = Inventory quantity / Shipments quantity.
Source: Ministry of Economy, Trade and Industry.

Figure 6.1
Trends in Indices on Mining and Manufacturing [1)]

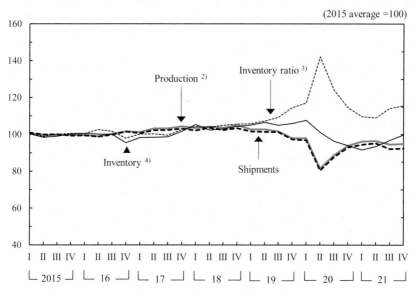

1) Seasonal adjustment indices. 2) Value added weights.
3) Inventory ratio = Inventory quantity / Shipments quantity. 4) End of the quarter.
Source: Ministry of Economy, Trade and Industry.

2. Principal Industries in the Manufacturing Sector

This section describes the major industries in the manufacturing sector. For each industry, (a) is described by the "Census of Manufacture 2020 (with 4 or more persons engaged)", and (b) is described by the "Indices on Mining and Manufacturing" (2015 average = 100).

(1) Machinery Industry

(A) Transport Equipment Industry

(a) In 2020, a total of 9,538 establishments employed 1,064,560 persons, and shipped 68.0 trillion yen worth of products in 2019.

(b) In 2021, production and shipments decreased by 0.8 percent and 0.9

percent, respectively, from the previous year, representing their third consecutive year of decrease. These decreases (in both production and shipments) were due to a decrease in "passenger cars", "ships and ship engines", etc.

(B) Production Machinery Industry

(a) In 2020, a total of 18,273 establishments employed 622,006 persons, and shipped 20.9 trillion yen worth of products in 2019.

(b) In 2021, production and shipments increased by 21.6 percent and 21.0 percent, respectively, from the previous year, representing their first increase in 3 years. The increase in production was due to an increase in "semiconductor and flat-panel display", "metal forming machinery", etc. The increase in shipments was due to an increase in "semiconductor and flat-panel display", "construction and mining machinery", etc.

(C) Electrical Machinery Industry

(a) In 2020, a total of 8,306 establishments employed 502,824 persons, and shipped 18.2 trillion yen worth of products in 2019.

(b) In 2021, production and shipments increased by 7.7 percent and 8.4 percent, respectively, from the previous year, representing their first increase in 3 years. These increases (in both production and shipments) were due to an increase in "switching devices", "electrical rotating machinery", etc.

(D) Electronic Parts and Devices Industry

(a) In 2020, a total of 3,789 establishments employed 410,504 persons, and shipped 14.1 trillion yen worth of products in 2019.

(b) In 2021, production and shipments increased by 14.5 percent and 12.7 percent, respectively, from the previous year. This marked the second consecutive year of increased production and the first increase in 3 years in shipments. The increase in production was due to an increase in "integrated circuits", "electronic devices", etc. The increase in shipments was due to an increase in "integrated circuits", "electronic parts", etc.

(E) General-Purpose Machinery Industry

(a) In 2020, a total of 6,615 establishments employed 327,541 persons, and shipped 12.2 trillion yen worth of products in 2019.

(b) In 2021, production and shipments increased by 12.1 percent and 13.4 percent, respectively, from the previous year, representing their first increase in 3 years. These increases (in both production and shipments) were due to an increase in "parts of general-purpose machinery", "pumps and compressors", etc.

(F) Information and Communication Electronics Equipment Industry

(a) In 2020, a total of 1,183 establishments employed 122,202 persons, and shipped 6.7 trillion yen worth of products in 2019.

(b) In 2021, production and shipments increased by 1.7 percent and 2.2 percent, respectively, from the previous year, representing their first increase in 2 years. These increases (in both production and shipments) were due to an increase in "radio communication equipment".

(2) Chemical Industry

(a) In 2020, a total of 4,650 establishments employed 381,259 persons, and shipped 29.3 trillion yen worth of products in 2019.

(b) In 2021, production and shipments increased by 3.5 percent and 2.8 percent, respectively, from the previous year, representing their first increase in 2 years. These increases (in both production and shipments) were due to an increase in "plastic", "petrochemical base products", etc.

(3) Iron and Steel Industry

(a) In 2020, a total of 4,015 establishments employed 223,524 persons, and shipped 17.7 trillion yen worth of products in 2019.

(b) In 2021, production and shipments increased by 15.7 percent and 13.7 percent, respectively, from the previous year, representing their first increase in 3 years. The increase in production was due to an increase in "hot rolled steel", "iron and steel crude products", etc. The increase in shipments was due to an increase in "hot rolled steel", "cold finished steel", etc.

(4) Fabricated Metals Industry

(a) In 2020, a total of 25,094 establishments employed 612,427 persons, and shipped 16.0 trillion yen worth of products in 2019.

(b) In 2021, production and shipments increased by 4.0 percent and 2.4 percent, respectively, from the previous year, representing their first increase in 3 years. These increases (in both production and shipments) were due to an increase in "cans", "metal products of building", etc.

3. Construction

The construction industry is indispensable in supporting the development of social capital, and fulfills a large role in building a vibrant future for Japan, such as through urban regeneration and regional revitalization. It also plays an extremely important role as a "local guardian" in disaster recovery, disaster prevention/reduction, deterioration countermeasures, etc.

Construction investments at nominal prices was on a declining trend after reaching a peak of 84 trillion yen in fiscal 1992, and fell to half of this peak (42 trillion yen) in fiscal 2010. Since then, they have been on a recovery trend due to such factors as the recovery from the Great East Japan Earthquake.

Construction investments in fiscal 2020 amounted to 60.9 trillion yen at nominal prices, down 2.5 percent compared to the previous fiscal year; they totaled 56.4 trillion yen at constant fiscal 2015 prices, down 2.4 percent from the previous fiscal year.

A breakdown of construction investment (nominal prices) shows that building construction totaled 37.5 trillion yen (down 6.8 percent from the previous fiscal year), while civil engineering works amounted to 23.4 trillion yen (up 5.1 percent).

In terms of public and private construction investment (nominal prices) in fiscal 2020, public investment amounted to 24.0 trillion yen (up 5.4 percent from the previous fiscal year), while private investment totaled 37.0 trillion yen (down 7.1 percent). Public investment accounted for 39.3 percent of total construction investment, while private investment accounted for 60.7 percent.

Table 6.3

Construction Investment (Nominal prices)

(Billion yen)

Item	FY2017	FY2018	FY2019*	FY2020*
Total	61,325	61,827	62,490	60,900
Building construction	40,859	40,486	40,260	37,540
Dwellings	17,563	17,258	16,710	15,570
Public sector	621	521	440	450
Private sector	16,942	16,737	16,270	15,120
Non-dwellings	15,686	15,399	15,650	14,680
Public sector	4,233	3,878	4,060	4,160
Private sector	11,453	11,522	11,590	10,520
Extension and renovation	7,610	7,828	7,900	7,290
Public sector	1,320	1,305	1,410	1,430
Private sector	6,291	6,523	6,490	5,860
Civil engineering works	20,466	21,342	22,230	23,360
Public sector	15,606	15,887	16,810	17,910
Private sector	4,860	5,455	5,420	5,450
Total				
Public investment	21,780	21,591	22,720	23,950
Private investment	39,545	40,236	39,770	36,950
Building construction				
Public investment	6,174	5,704	5,910	6,040
Private investment	34,686	34,782	34,350	31,500
Civil engineering works				
Public investment	15,606	15,887	16,810	17,910
Private investment	4,860	5,455	5,420	5,450

Source: Ministry of Land, Infrastructure, Transport and Tourism.

In 2021, the number of new construction starts for dwellings (in the case of apartment buildings, the number of apartment units) increased 5.0 percent from the previous year to 0.86 million units, the first increase in 5 years, as occupier-owned housing units, housing units for rent, and housing units built for sale all increased.

The floor space (public and private) of the entire building whose construction started in 2021 was 122.24 million square meters, up 7.5 percent compared to the previous year.

Table 6.4
Building Construction Started by Types of Investor, Dwellings and Industries, and Structure

Types	Floor space (1,000 m^2)		Construction cost (billion yen)	
	2020	2021	2020	2021
Total	113,744	122,239	24,307	26,261
Investor				
Public	5,381	5,372	1,771	1,762
Private	108,363	116,866	22,535	24,499
Dwellings and Industries				
Dwelling	69,508	73,779	14,047	14,954
Non-dwelling	44,236	48,460	10,259	11,306
Structure				
Wooden	49,756	53,100	8,560	9,148
Non-wooden	63,987	69,138	15,746	17,112

Source: Ministry of Land, Infrastructure, Transport and Tourism.

Chapter 7
Energy

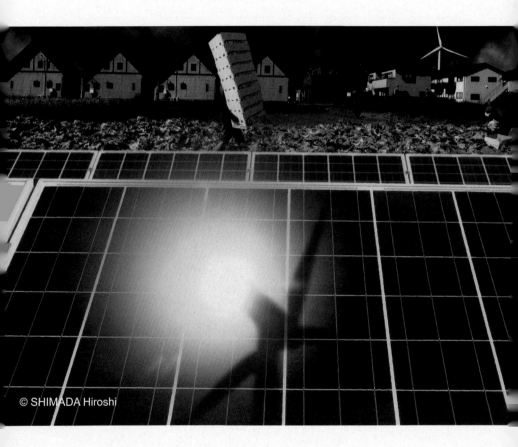

© SHIMADA Hiroshi

The blessings of nature. Japan is expanding adoption of renewable energy such as photovoltaic and wind power to reduce greenhouse gas emissions and improve energy self-sufficiency. Domestic supply of primary energy from renewables (including hydroelectricity) has increased for 8 consecutive years.

1. Supply and Demand

Japan is dependent on imports for 88.8 percent of its energy supply. Since experiencing the two oil crises of the 1970s, Japan has taken measures to promote energy conservation, introduce alternatives to petroleum such as nuclear power, natural gas, coal, etc., and secure a stable supply of petroleum through stockpiling and other measures. As a result, its dependence on petroleum declined from 75.5 percent in fiscal 1973 to 40.3 percent in fiscal 2010. However, since the Great East Japan Earthquake, the percentage of fossil fuels has been increasing, as a substitute for nuclear power as fuel for power generation. The level of dependence on petroleum, which had been on a declining trend, increased to 44.5 percent in fiscal 2012. However, it is once again on a declining trend as the switch to LNG power and renewable energy progresses.

In fiscal 2020, the domestic supply of primary energy in Japan was 17,965 petajoules, down 6.1 percent from the previous fiscal year. Its breakdown was: 36.4 percent in petroleum, 24.6 percent in coal, 23.8 percent in natural gas and city gas, 3.7 percent in hydro power, and 1.8 percent in nuclear power. Other sources were also used, including energy from waste, geothermal, and natural energy (photovoltaic, wind power, biomass energy, etc.).

Energy units

Joule (J) is employed as a common unit (International System of Units: SI) for energy across all energy sources in presenting international statistical information. The unit Petajoule (PJ: 10^{15} or quadrillion joules), etc. is used here to reduce the number of digits. The energy of one kiloliter of petroleum is calculated using the following formulae:

$$1 \text{ kiloliter of petroleum} = 3.87 \times 10^{10} \text{ joules}$$
$$1 \text{ gigajoule} = 10^{9} \text{ joules}$$
$$1 \text{ petajoule} = 10^{15} \text{ joules}$$
$$1 \text{ exajoule} = 10^{18} \text{ joules}$$

Petroleum is traded internationally using the volume unit of barrels. One barrel equals approximately 158.987 liters.

The government has been working to construct a new energy supply-demand structure oriented toward stable supply of energy and lowering energy costs. In this process, energy-saving and renewable energy that takes global warming into consideration has been introduced, and aims are being made toward reducing dependency on nuclear power.

Figure 7.1
Domestic Supply of Primary Energy by Energy Source [1]

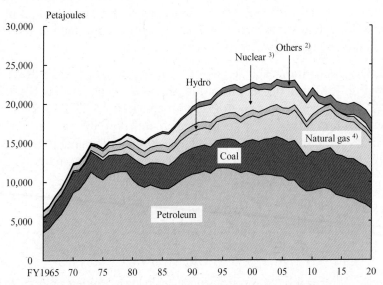

1) A different statistical method was used for the figures since FY1990. 2) Photovoltaic, wind power, geothermal energy, etc. 3) In fiscal 2014, the domestic supply of nuclear energy was zero due to the suspended operation of all nuclear power plants in Japan. 4) Natural gas and city gas.
Source: Agency for Natural Resources and Energy

Table 7.1
Trends in Domestic Supply of Primary Energy and Percentage by Energy Source

(Petajoules)

Item	FY2005	FY2010	FY2015	FY2019	FY2020
Domestic supply of primary energy ..	22,905	21,995	20,016	19,136	17,965
Energy self-sufficiency (%) [1]	19.6	20.2	7.3	12.0	11.2
Petroleum	10,691	8,858	8,138	7,101	6,543
Coal	4,782	4,997	5,154	4,848	4,419
Natural gas and city gas	3,291	3,995	4,657	4,281	4,272
Hydro	671	716	726	676	666
Nuclear	2,660	2,462	79	539	328
Others [2]	809	966	1,262	1,692	1,736
Percentage					
Petroleum	46.7	40.3	40.7	37.1	36.4
Coal	20.9	22.7	25.8	25.3	24.6
Natural gas and city gas	14.4	18.2	23.3	22.4	23.8
Hydro	2.9	3.3	3.6	3.5	3.7
Nuclear	11.6	11.2	0.4	2.8	1.8
Others [2]	3.5	4.4	6.3	8.8	9.7

1) Domestic production of primary energy (including nuclear) / Domestic supply of primary energy × 100. 2) Photovoltaic, wind power, geothermal energy, etc.
Source: Agency for Natural Resources and Energy.

Figure 7.2
International Comparison of Energy Consumption/GDP [1] (2018)

(Japan = 1)

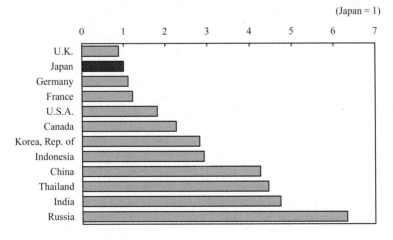

1) Primary energy consumption (tons of oil equivalent) / Real GDP (2010 U.S. dollars).
Source: Agency for Natural Resources and Energy.

Energy consumption per GDP is lower in Japan than in other industrialized countries. This indicates that Japan is one of the most energy-efficient countries in the world.

Energy consumption in Japan was suppressed due to greater energy conservation brought on by two oil shocks in the 1970s. After that, consumption increased until the 1990s due to a decrease in crude oil prices. However, in the 2000s, as crude oil prices rose again, final energy consumption peaked in fiscal 2005, and then started decreasing. In fiscal 2020, real GDP was lower than in fiscal 2019, which added to a decrease in final energy consumption.

Figure 7.3
Trends in Final Energy Consumption and Real GDP [1]

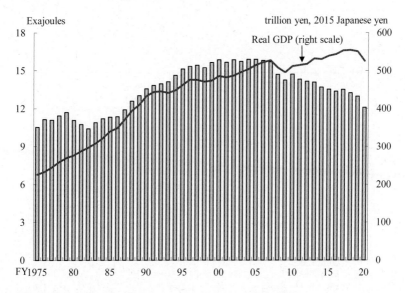

1) A different statistical method was used for the figures since FY1990.
Source: Cabinet Office; Agency for Natural Resources and Energy.

Final energy consumption in fiscal 2020 decreased 6.7 percent from the previous fiscal year, and even by sector, it has decreased in the industry sector, commercial industry sector, and transportation sector.

Figure 7.4
Trends in Final Energy Consumption by Sector [1]

Exajoules

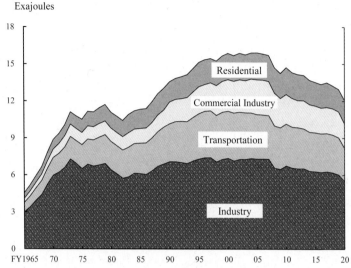

1) A different statistical method was used for the figures since FY1990.
Source: Agency for Natural Resources and Energy.

Figure 7.5
Final Energy Consumption by Country (2019)

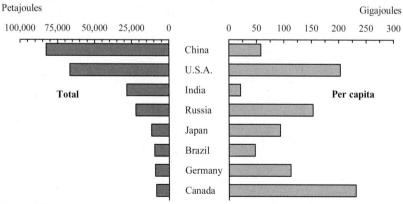

Source: United Nations.

2. Electric Power

Approximately half of Japan's primary energy supply of petroleum, coal and other energy sources is converted into electric power.

Electricity output (including in-house power generation) in Japan totaled 949 billion kWh in fiscal 2020, down 2.2 percent from the previous fiscal year. Of this total, thermal power accounted for 83.2 percent; hydro power, 9.1 percent; nuclear power, 3.9 percent.

Table 7.2

Trends in Electricity Output and Power Consumption [1]

(Million kWh)

Item	FY2005	FY2010	FY2015	FY2019	FY2020
Electricity Output					
Total	1,157,926	1,156,888	1,024,179	970,771	948,979
Thermal	761,841	771,306	908,779	792,810	789,725
Hydro	86,350	90,681	91,383	86,314	86,310
Nuclear	304,755	288,230	9,437	61,035	37,011
Others [2]	4,980	6,671	14,580	30,612	35,933
Percentage					
Total	100.0	100.0	100.0	100.0	100.0
Thermal	65.8	66.7	88.7	81.7	83.2
Hydro	7.5	7.8	8.9	8.9	9.1
Nuclear	26.3	24.9	0.9	6.3	3.9
Others [2]	0.4	0.6	1.4	3.2	3.8
Electricity Power Consumption [3]					
Total	1,043,800	1,056,441	955,345	952,745	935,491
Generated by electric power suppliers	918,265	931,059	841,542	877,133	863,159
Consumption of in-house generation	125,535	125,382	113,803	75,612	72,332

1) Including in-house generation. 2) Photovoltaic, wind power, geothermal energy, etc.
3) Changes were made to the categorization of Electricity Suppliers since FY2019.
Source: Agency for Natural Resources and Energy.

3. Gas

Gas production was 1,574 petajoules in fiscal 2020, down 3.2 percent from the previous fiscal year. Of this total, natural gas plus vaporized liquefied natural gas accounted for 96.4 percent; and the remaining 3.6 percent was made up of petroleum gases, such as vaporized liquefied petroleum gas and other petroleum-based gas. Gas purchases for fiscal 2020 totaled 627 petajoules.

Gas sales for fiscal 2020 totaled 1,654 petajoules, or a year-on-year drop of 2.3 percent. Of this total, 57.6 percent was sold to industry, 25.4 percent to residential use, and 9.2 percent to the commercial sector.

Table 7.3

Trends in Production and Purchases, and Sales of Gas [1) 2)]

(Petajoules)

Item	FY2010		FY2015		FY2019		FY2020	
Production and purchases [3]	1,547		1,610		2,247		2,200	
Production	1,288	(100.0)	1,372	(100.0)	1,625	(100.0)	1,574	(100.0)
Petroleum gases [4)	46	(3.6)	48	(3.5)	58	(3.5)	57	(3.6)
Natural gas and								
vaporized liquefied natural gas [5) ..	1,241	(96.4)	1,324	(96.5)	1,568	(96.5)	1,517	(96.4)
Others	...	(...)	...	(...)	...	(...)	...	(...)
Purchases	259	(100.0)	238	(100.0)	622	(100.0)	627	(100.0)
Petroleum gases [6)	6	(2.4)	3	(1.1)	...	(...)	...	(...)
Natural gas and								
vaporized liquefied natural gas	253	(97.6)	236	(98.9)	617	(99.1)	621	(99.1)
Others	0	(0.0)	0	(0.0)	0	(0.0)	0	(0.0)
Sales	1,477	(100.0)	1,526	(100.0)	1,692	(100.0)	1,654	(100.0)
Residential	410	(27.7)	387	(25.3)	392	(23.2)	419	(25.4)
Commercial	198	(13.4)	177	(11.6)	174	(10.3)	153	(9.2)
Industrial	738	(50.0)	842	(55.2)	998	(59.0)	953	(57.6)
Others	131	(8.9)	120	(7.9)	128	(7.5)	129	(7.8)

1) Figures in parentheses indicate a percentage. 2) A different statistical method was used for the figures since 2019. 3) Since there are some concealed sources, the breakdown totals may not match the overall totals. 4) Figures up until FY2015 are a total of volatile oil gas, liquefied petroleum gas, and other petroleum-based gas. Starting FY2019, figures are a total of vaporized liquefied petroleum gas and other petroleum-based gas.
5) Figures up until FY2015 are a total of natural gas and liquefied natural gas. 6) Vaporized liquefied petroleum gas, other petroleum-based gas.

Source: The Japan Gas Association.

Chapter 8

Science and Technology/

Information and Communication

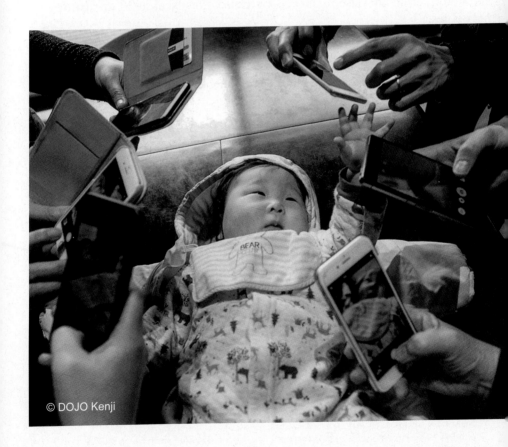

© DOJO Kenji

According to the "2021 Communications Usage Trend Survey", the ratio of personal ownership of smartphones is 74.3 percent. Smartphones have surpassed personal computers as personal devices for Internet use, and are used by approximately 90 percent of each age group in the range 20–49. The ratio of individuals using social media has reached 78.7 percent.

1. Science and Technology

(1) Researchers and R&D Expenditures

Japan's expenditures for the research and development (R&D) of science and technology are at a top level among major countries, and support the technology-based nation of Japan. Researchers in the fields of science and technology (including social sciences and humanities) as of the end of March 2021 totaled 890,500. The total R&D expenditures in fiscal 2020 amounted to 19.2 trillion yen, a decrease of 1.7 percent from the previous fiscal year. Relative to GDP, R&D expenditures was 3.59 percent, a 0.08 percentage point increase from the previous fiscal year.

Table 8.1

Trends in Researchers and Expenditures on R&D

Fiscal year	Number of Researchers [1)2)]	Females (%)	R&D expenditures (billion yen)	GDP (billion yen)	Ratio of R&D expenditures to GDP (%)
2011	844,400	14.0	17,379	500,041	3.48
2012	835,700	14.4	17,325	499,424	3.47
2013	841,600	14.6	18,134	512,686	3.54
2014	866,900	14.7	18,971	523,418	3.62
2015	847,100	15.3	18,939	540,739	3.50
2016	853,700	15.7	18,433	544,827	3.38
2017	867,000	16.2	19,050	555,722	3.43
2018	874,800	16.6	19,526	556,304	3.51
2019	881,000	16.9	19,576	557,307	3.51
2020	890,500	17.5	19,237	535,510	3.59

1) As of the end of each fiscal year. 2) Business enterprises, non-profit institutions and public organizations: Prorated by the percentage of time that researchers are actually engaged in R&D activities. Universities and colleges: headcount.

Source: Statistics Bureau, MIC.

As of the end of March 2021, the number of researchers amounted to 515,500 persons in business enterprises, 38,200 persons in non-profit institutions and public organizations, and 336,800 persons in universities and colleges. In terms of R&D expenditures in fiscal 2020, business enterprises spent 13.9 trillion yen (72.1 percent of total R&D expenditures), non-profit institutions and public organizations spent 1.7 trillion yen (8.8 percent), and universities and colleges spent 3.7 trillion yen (19.1 percent).

Universities and colleges spent more than 90 percent of their R&D expenditure on natural sciences and engineering for basic research and applied research, while business enterprises allocated over 70 percent for development purposes.

With regard to the portion in the R&D expenditures in fiscal 2020 by specific objective, 3.1 trillion yen went to the life sciences field (16.0 percent of total R&D expenditures), 2.5 trillion yen (13.2 percent) to the information technology field, 1.1 trillion yen (5.5 percent) to the environmental science and technology field and 1.0 trillion yen (5.2 percent) to the materials field, etc.

Approximately 89 percent of the 515,500 researchers at business enterprises at the end of March 2021, or 459,600 persons, were in the manufacturing industries; the largest number was in the motor vehicles, parts and accessories industry, followed by the information and communication electronics equipment industry, then by the electronic parts, devices and electronic circuits industry.

In terms of R&D expenditures in fiscal 2020, of 13.9 trillion yen spent by business enterprises, 12.5 trillion yen was spent by manufacturing industries. The motor vehicles, parts and accessories industry spent the most, followed by the medicines industry, then by the electronic parts, devices and electronic circuits industry.

Figure 8.1
Researchers and Expenditures by Industry (Business enterprises)

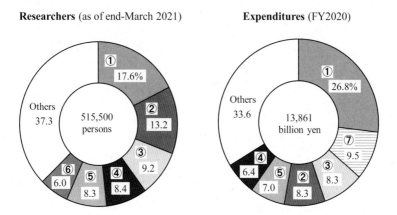

Researchers (as of end-March 2021)   Expenditures (FY2020)

① Motor vehicles, parts and accessories ② Information and communication electronics equipment
③ Electronic parts, devices and electronic circuits ④ Business oriented machinery
⑤ Chemical products ⑥ Electrical machinery, equipment and supplies ⑦ Medicines
Source: Statistics Bureau, MIC.

(2) Technology Balance of Payments (Technology Trade)

Technology trade is defined as the export or import of technology by business enterprises with other countries, such as patents, expertise, and technical guidance. In fiscal 2020, Japan earned 3,101.0 billion yen from technology exports, which was down 15.3 percent from the previous fiscal year. This was the third consecutive decrease. Of the total receipts, 70.3 percent was from overseas parent/subsidiary companies. Meanwhile, payments to technology imports stood at 559.8 billion yen, an increase of 3.0 percent compared with the previous fiscal year. It increased for the first time in 3 years. Of this figure, 36.7 percent was for payments to overseas parent/subsidiary companies.

Table 8.2

Technology Trade by Business Enterprises

Fiscal year	Exports Value (billion yen)	Exports Annual increase rate (%)	Imports Value (billion yen)	Imports Annual increase rate (%)	Exports value / Imports value
2011	2,385.2	-2.1	414.8	-21.8	5.75
2012	2,721.0	14.1	448.6	8.2	6.07
2013	3,395.2	24.8	577.7	28.8	5.88
2014	3,660.3	7.8	513.0	-11.2	7.13
2015	3,949.8	7.9	602.6	17.5	6.55
2016	3,571.9	-9.6	452.9	-24.8	7.89
2017	3,884.4	8.7	629.8	39.1	6.17
2018	3,871.1	-0.3	591.0	-6.2	6.55
2019	3,662.6	-5.4	543.6	-8.0	6.74
2020	3,101.0	-15.3	559.8	3.0	5.54

Source: Statistics Bureau, MIC.

In fiscal 2020, Japan exported 3,101.0 billion yen of technologies; major export destinations were: the U.S.A. (1,182.7 billion yen, or 38.1 percent of total exports), followed by China (485.3 billion yen), the U.K. (301.7 billion yen), and Thailand (271.0 billion yen). On the other hand, Japan imported 559.8 billion yen of technologies, mainly from the U.S.A. (392.4 billion yen, or 70.1 percent of total imports), followed by Switzerland (34.3 billion yen), the Netherlands (25.1 billion yen) and Germany (24.2 billion yen).

Figure 8.2
Composition of Technology Trade by Major Country (FY2020)

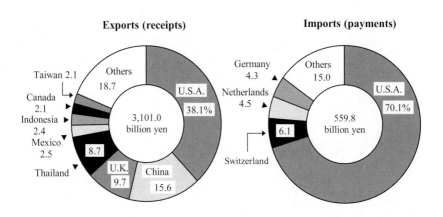

Source: Statistics Bureau, MIC.

2. Patents

The total number of patent applications remained robust in and after 1998 as more than 400,000 applications were filed every year, but a gradual drop has been seen since 2006. The level remained above 300,000 applications for some time. However, the number of applications in 2020 was 288,472, down 6.33 percent from the previous year.

Table 8.3
Patents

					(Cases)
Item	2000	2005	2010	2015	2020
Applications	436,865	427,078	344,598	318,721	288,472
Registrations	125,880	122,944	222,693	189,358	179,383
Existing vested rights	1,040,607	1,123,055	1,423,432	1,946,568	2,039,040

Source: Japan Patent Office.

Table 8.4
PCT International Applications by Country

Country	2018	2019	2020*	Change from 2019 (%)
Total	252,779	265,381	275,900	4.0
China	53,445	59,193	68,720	16.1
U.S.A.	56,172	57,499	59,230	3.0
Japan	49,703	52,693	50,520	-4.1
Korea, Rep. of	16,919	19,073	20,060	5.2
Germany	19,754	19,358	18,643	-3.7
France	7,922	7,906	7,904	0.0
U.K.	5,637	5,773	5,912	2.4
Switzerland	4,596	4,627	4,883	5.5
Sweden	4,175	4,202	4,356	3.7
Netherlands	4,132	4,055	4,035	-0.5

Source: World Intellectual Property Organization.

Over 150 countries, including Japan, have joined the international patent system of the World Intellectual Property Organization (WIPO) as of February 2022. In 2020, the number of international patent applications filed under the Patent Cooperation Treaty (PCT) was 275,900, of which 50,520 were from Japan, accounting for 18.3 percent.

The United States Patent and Trademark Office ranked first among major patent offices for applications filed by Japanese applicants in 2020, with 79,207 applications. The number of patent applications filed by Japanese applicants at the China National Intellectual Property Administration was 47,862.

Figure 8.3
Changes in Patent Applications with Major Offices by Japanese Applicants

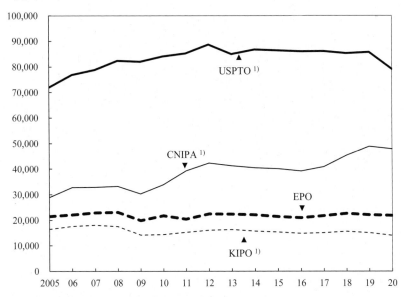

1) The USPTO, CNIPA and KIPO data for 2020 are provisional.
USPTO: United States Patent and Trademark Office; CNIPA: China National Intellectual Property Administration; EPO: European Patent Office; KIPO: Korean Intellectual Property Office.
Source: Japan Patent Office.

3. Information and Communication

(1) Diffusion of the Internet

The ratio of individuals using the Internet, of which commercial usage started in 1993, exceeded 80 percent in 2013. At the end of August 2021, the ratio of individuals who had used the Internet in the past year (individuals who are 6 years of age and older) was 82.9 percent. According to the individual Internet usage rate by age group, the usage rate exceeded 90 percent in each age group between 13 and 59 years old.

Figure 8.4
Trends in Internet Usage Rate by Age Group [1]

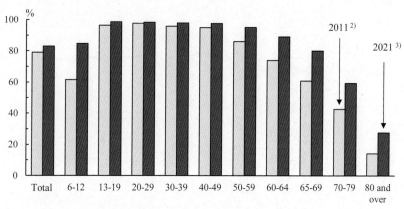

1) Ages 6 years and over. 2) End of 2011. 3) End of August 2021.
Source: Ministry of Internal Affairs and Communications.

According to the status of Internet use by device by age group as of the end of August 2021, the usage rate of smartphones was the highest (68.5 percent), followed by computers (48.1 percent). Figures for the rate of Internet use by device by age group show that more than 80 percent use smartphones in each age group between 13 and 59 years old.

Table 8.5
Status of Internet Use by Device by Age Group (2021)

(%)

Item	Usage rate	6-12 years	13-19	20-29	30-39	40-49	50-59	60-69	70-79	80 and over
Smartphones	68.5	40.5	80.6	89.8	91.7	88.2	83.9	70.0	40.6	12.1
Computers	48.1	25.5	45.8	65.6	62.5	63.5	62.6	48.8	28.2	10.3
Tablets	25.1	47.9	36.8	31.4	34.2	31.2	27.1	19.4	8.8	2.8
Mobile phones [1]	10.4	5.6	8.5	10.6	9.0	11.0	12.5	11.9	12.0	7.8

1) Cell phones and PHS (Personal Handyphone System).
Source: Ministry of Internal Affairs and Communications.

As of the end of August 2021, 51.9 percent of enterprises had introduced telework. This marked an increase of 4.4 percentage points compared with the previous year. The most frequent telework pattern was working from home, 91.5 percent, followed by mobile work, 30.5 percent and working from a satellite office, 15.2 percent.

(2) Progress of Communication Technologies

As of the end of March 2021, those with subscriptions for 3.9-4G mobile phones (LTE) made up the largest segment of broadband (connection) subscribers, amounting to 154 million subscriptions. Those with BWA (Broadband Wireless Access) service (access service connecting to networks via broadband wireless access systems using the 2.5GHz band [WiMAX, etc.]) was the second highest, with 76 million subscribers.

Meanwhile, IP phone services (voice phone services that use Internet Protocol technology across part or all of the communication network), which use broadband circuits as access lines, entered full-scale use between 2002 and 2003. As of the end of March 2021, the total number of IP phone subscribers was 45 million.

Table 8.6
Subscribers to Telecommunications Services [1]

(Thousands)

Item	2017	2018	2019	2020	2021
Public phones (NTT [2] only)	161	158	155	151	146
Fixed phone services	19,868	18,450	17,242	15,954	14,856
Mobile phones [3]	166,853	172,790	179,873	186,514	195,055
IP phone	40,985	42,555	43,413	44,131	44,670
ISDN (Integrated Services Digital Network)	3,116	2,904	2,715	2,507	2,307
DSL (Digital Subscriber Line)	2,512	2,146	1,730	1,398	1,073
Cable Internet	6,847	6,880	6,837	6,712	6,584
FTTH (Fiber To The Home)	29,456	30,604	31,669	33,085	35,017
BWA (Broadband Wireless Access) ..	47,888	58,226	66,241	71,200	75,704
3.9-4G mobile phones (LTE)	102,942	120,727	136,642	152,623	154,366
International phone calls, sent and received	472,200	493,400	448,500	471,400	367,600

1) End of March. 2) Nippon Telegraph and Telephone Corporation.
3) Cell phones and PHS (Personal Handyphone System).
Source: Ministry of Internal Affairs and Communications.

In 2020, the number of fixed-broadband subscribers in Japan was 44 million, the third-largest after China, 484 million and the U.S.A., 121 million.

Figure 8.5
International Comparison of Fixed-Broadband Subscribers (2020)

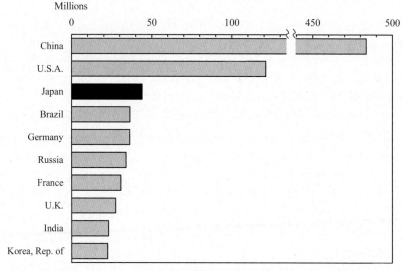

Source: International Telecommunication Union.

(3) Telephones

The number of fixed phone service subscription contracts has continued to decrease in recent years. As of the end of March 2021, the number of fixed phone subscribers was 15 million (down 6.9 percent from the previous year). Meanwhile, the number of mobile phone subscribers (cell phones and personal handyphone systems) totaled 187 million at the end of March 2020, marking a rise by 4.6 percent year-on-year to 195 million at the end of March 2021.

Figure 8.6
Telephone Service Subscribers [1]

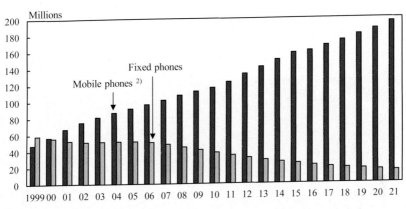

1) End of March. 2) Subscribers of cell phones and PHS (Personal Handyphone System).
Source: Ministry of Internal Affairs and Communications.

(4) Postal Service

As of the end of March 2022, Japan Post Co., Ltd. had 24,284 post offices nationwide. In fiscal 2021, post offices handled 19.2 billion items of domestic mail (including parcels), which was a 2.3 percent decrease from the previous fiscal year. Furthermore, the total quantity of international mail (letters, Express Mail Services [EMS], and parcels) sent in fiscal 2021 amounted to 24.7 million items, an increase of 7.5 percent from the previous fiscal year.

Table 8.7
Postal Services

(Millions)

Item	FY2000	FY2005	FY2010	FY2015	FY2020	FY2021
Domestic						
Letters	26,114.4	22,666.1	19,757.9	17,981.0	15,221.0	14,833.1
Parcels	310.5	2,075.0	2,968.4	4,052.4	4,390.1	4,334.9
International						
Sent	106.0	77.5	54.2	48.9	23.0	24.7
Letters [1]	104.3	76.1	52.8	44.1	20.6	21.9
Parcels	1.7	1.5	1.4	4.8	2.5	2.8

1) Including Express Mail Services (EMS).
Source: Japan Post Co., Ltd.

Chapter 9

Transport

© KAWAHARA Yuta

Where to today? People were asked to stay home to help prevent the spread of COVID-19, and could no longer move freely inside or outside Japan. Many are eagerly awaiting the day when they can enjoy travel as before.

1. Domestic Transport

Various modes of domestic transport are used in Japan; almost all passenger transport is by railway, while nearly all freight transport is by motor vehicle and cargo ship.

Figure 9.1
Composition of Domestic Transport

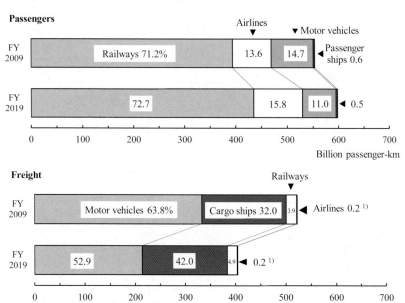

1) Including overweight baggage and postal mail.
Source: Ministry of Land, Infrastructure, Transport and Tourism.

(1) Domestic Passenger Transport

No major changes have been observed in recent years in the volume of domestic passenger transport. Under these circumstances, a shift from private automobiles to public transportation should be promoted as a measure against global warming, along with promotion of the development and distribution of environment-friendly vehicles and measures for traffic flow improvement. Therefore, in addition to the promotion of computerization, such as adoption of IC cards (multiple-use IC [integrated circuit] cards) and increased convenience in public transportation through the improvement of transfers, workplace "eco-commuting" measures have been promoted.

In fiscal 2019, the number of domestic transport passengers was 31.17 billion (down 1.0 percent from the previous fiscal year). The total volume of passenger transport was 598.19 billion passenger-kilometers (down 2.1 percent).

Table 9.1
Domestic Passenger Transport

Item	Passengers carried (millions)		Passenger kilometers (millions)	
	FY2018	FY2019	FY2018	FY2019
Total transport volume	31,498	31,172	611,250	598,185
Railways	25,269	25,190	441,614	435,063
JR (Japan Railways)	9,556	9,503	277,670	271,936
Other than JR	15,714	15,687	163,944	163,126
Motor vehicles	6,037	5,800	70,101	65,556
Buses (Commercial use)	4,646	4,532	64,108	60,070
Taxis and limousine hires	1,391	1,268	5,993	5,486
Airlines	104	102	96,171	94,490
Passenger ships	88	80	3,364	3,076

Source: Ministry of Land, Infrastructure, Transport and Tourism.

In fiscal 2019, the Japan Railways (JR) group reported 9.50 billion passengers (down 0.6 percent from the previous fiscal year) and 271.94 billion passenger-kilometers (down 2.1 percent). Railways other than JR reported 15.69 billion passengers (down 0.2 percent) and 163.13 billion passenger-kilometers (down 0.5 percent).

To promote the use of buses, approaches to improve punctuality and speed using bus lanes and to make buses more convenient, such as by introducing a bus location system that provides locational information of buses as well as an IC card system that enables smooth bus rides, are being carried out. Commercial buses transported 4.53 billion passengers (down 2.4 percent from the previous fiscal year) and 60.07 billion passenger-kilometers (down 6.3 percent); both figures of passengers and passenger-kilometers declined in fiscal 2019.

In recent years, the development of aviation networks has been underway, such as through enhancing the functions of metropolitan airports and promoting the entry of LCCs, in order to strengthen Japan's international competitiveness in both business and tourism. In promoting the entry of LCCs, there are expectations for creation of new demand, such as through the expansion of foreign tourists visiting Japan as well as of domestic tourism. Fiscal 2019 air transport records show that there were 102 million passengers (down 2.0 percent from the previous fiscal year), and passenger-kilometers amounted to 94.49 billion (down 1.7 percent).

In fiscal 2019, passenger ships reported 80 million passengers (down 8.5 percent from the previous fiscal year) and 3.08 billion passenger-kilometers (down 8.6 percent).

(2) Domestic Freight Transport

In the area of domestic freight, a total of 4.71 billion metric tons (down 0.3 percent from the previous fiscal year) of freight was transported for a total of 404.44 billion ton-kilometers (down 1.3 percent) in fiscal 2019. As for transport tonnage volume in fiscal 2019, motor vehicle transport accounted for more than 90 percent of the total.

Table 9.2
Domestic Freight Transport

Item	Freight tonnage (thousands)		Ton kilometers (millions)	
	FY2018	FY2019	FY2018	FY2019
Total transport volume	4,727,467	4,714,117	409,902	404,440
Railways	42,321	42,660	19,369	19,993
Motor vehicles	4,329,784	4,329,132	210,467	213,836
Commercial use	3,018,819	3,053,766	182,490	186,377
Non-commercial use	1,310,965	1,275,366	27,977	27,459
Cargo ships	354,445	341,450	179,089	169,680
Airlines [1]	917	875	977	931

1) Including overweight baggage and postal mail.
Source: Ministry of Land, Infrastructure, Transport and Tourism.

2. International Transport

(1) International Passenger Transport

The global economic downturn after September 2008, the spread of a new influenza in early 2009, and the effects of the Great East Japan Earthquake in 2011 reduced international air passenger transport on Japanese airlines. In 2012, this trend reversed to an increase, and the increase continued for 7 consecutive years until 2019. However, due to the effects of the COVID-19 pandemic, Japanese airlines transported 4.36 million passengers (down 81.4 percent from the previous year) and registered 22.55 billion passenger kilometers (down 78.5 percent) in 2020.

The number of Japanese overseas travelers in 2021 was 512,200 (down 83.9 percent from the previous year). The number of foreign visitors to Japan totaled 245,900 (down 94.0 percent from the previous year), a sharp decline resulting from the outbreak of COVID-19.

Figure 9.2
Japanese Overseas Travelers and Foreign Visitor Arrivals

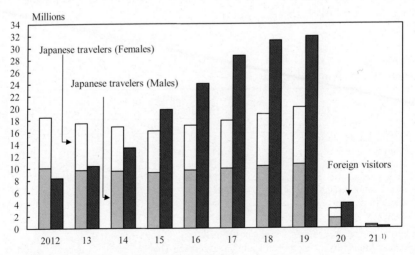

1) The Foreign visitors data for 2021 is provisional.
Source: Immigration Services Agency of Japan; Japan National Tourism Organization.

According to reports on arrivals by tourist offices in countries around the world, the U.S.A. and the Republic of Korea had many Japanese visitors in 2019.

Table 9.3
Japanese Overseas Travelers by Destination

Country or area of destination	2017		2018		2019	
	Number of arrivals	Annual change (%)	Number of arrivals	Annual change (%)	Number of arrivals	Annual change (%)
U.S.A. [1)2)]	3,595,607	-0.2	3,493,313	-2.8	3,752,980	7.4
Korea, Rep. of [3)]	2,311,447	0.6	2,948,527	27.6	3,271,706	11.0
China [3)]	2,680,033	3.6	2,689,662	0.4	...	...
Taiwan [4)]	1,898,854	0.2	1,969,151	3.7	2,167,952	10.1
Thailand [5)]	1,544,442	7.3	1,655,996	7.2	...	...
Hong Kong SAR [2)]	813,207	17.4	852,192	4.8	660,883	-22.4
Germany [6)]	584,871	7.3	613,248	4.9	614,638	0.2
Spain [2)]	444,518	-4.1	547,182	23.1	677,659	23.8

1) Including territories and dependencies (Northern Mariana Islands, Guam, American Samoa, Puerto Rico and United States Virgin Islands, etc.). 2) Arrivals of non-resident tourists at national borders, by country of residence. 3) Arrivals of non-resident visitors at national borders, by nationality. 4) Arrivals of non-resident visitors at national borders, by country of residence. 5) Arrivals of non-resident tourists at national borders, by nationality. 6) Arrivals of non-resident tourists in all types of accommodation establishments, by country of residence.
Source: Japan National Tourism Organization.

The number of foreign visitors to Japan in 2021 broken down by country/region, the number of visitors from Asian countries was highest, totaling 150,427 (down 94.0 percent from the previous year). Among Asian countries, the number of visitors from China was highest, amounting to 42,239, and the figure accounted for 17.2 percent of the total number of foreign visitors to Japan.

As part of measures to prevent the spread of COVID-19, travel across international borders was limited. This led to a sharp decline in the number of foreign visitors to Japan, reaching the lowest number since 1964 in 2021.

Table 9.4
Foreign Visitors

Region, country or area of origin	2019		2020		2021*	
	Number of arrivals	Percentage distribution	Number of arrivals	Percentage distribution	Number of arrivals	Percentage distribution
Total arrivals [1]	31,882,049	100.0	4,115,828	100.0	245,862	100.0
Asia	26,819,278	84.1	3,403,547	82.7	150,427	61.2
China	9,594,394	30.1	1,069,256	26.0	42,239	17.2
Viet Nam	495,051	1.6	152,559	3.7	26,586	10.8
Korea, Rep. of	5,584,597	17.5	487,939	11.9	18,947	7.7
India	175,896	0.6	26,931	0.7	8,831	3.6
Philippines	613,114	1.9	109,110	2.7	5,625	2.3
Indonesia	412,779	1.3	77,724	1.9	5,209	2.1
Europe	1,986,529	6.2	240,897	5.9	52,238	21.2
U.K.	424,279	1.3	51,024	1.2	7,294	3.0
Africa	55,039	0.2	7,840	0.2	6,769	2.8
North America	2,187,557	6.9	284,829	6.9	26,238	10.7
U.S.A.	1,723,861	5.4	219,307	5.3	20,026	8.1
Canada	375,262	1.2	53,365	1.3	3,536	1.4
South America	111,200	0.3	18,222	0.4	5,204	2.1
Oceania	721,718	2.3	160,386	3.9	4,953	2.0
Australia	621,771	2.0	143,508	3.5	3,265	1.3

1) Including stateless people, etc.
Source: Japan National Tourism Organization.

In 2021, of the total number of foreign visitors to Japan, tourists numbered 66,387 people, or 27.0 percent of total foreign visitors. The highest number of tourists came from U.S.A., with 7,993 travelers, followed by U.K., with 4,538 travelers.

(2) International Freight Transport

The volume of seaborne foreign transport in 2020 was 889 million tons, down 7.3 percent over the previous year. Of this figure, total exports decreased by 9.6 percent to 58 million tons, and total imports decreased by 13.4 percent to 435 million tons.

Table 9.5
Seaborne Foreign Transport

(Thousand tons)

Year	Total	Exports	Imports	Cross Transport
2000	739,377	34,960	538,875	165,542
2005	777,869	45,404	529,239	203,225
2010	819,075	44,758	465,898	308,419
2015	1,056,144	60,802	544,702	450,639
2019	959,693	64,609	502,079	393,006
2020*	889,365	58,411	435,019	395,935

Source: Ministry of Land, Infrastructure, Transport and Tourism.

Air-shipped international freight in 2020 totaled 1.28 million tons in terms of volume (down 11.2 percent from the previous year) and 7.27 billion tons in terms of ton-kilometers (down 9.9 percent).

Chapter 10

Commerce

© Statistics Bureau, MIC

A neighborhood rice shop. According to the "2016 Economic Census for Business Activity", there were 9,792 rice, barley and other cereals stores as of June 1, 2016.

1. Wholesale and Retail

The "2016 Economic Census for Business Activity" showed that 1.36 million wholesale and retail establishments were in operation in Japan. The number of persons engaged at such establishments became 11.84 million. Sales in the wholesale and retail industries amounted to 500.79 trillion yen, accounting for 30.8 percent of the total of all industries.

(1) Wholesale Trade

The number of wholesale establishments in operation was 364,814 in 2016. Observed by size of operation in terms of persons engaged, establishments with less than 20 persons accounted for 88.6 percent of the total. By type of corporate form, 88.5 percent of them were corporations, while 11.4 percent were individual proprietorships.

Table 10.1
Establishments and Persons Engaged in the Wholesale and Retail Sector (2016)

Item	Total	Wholesale	Retail
Number of Establishments	1,355,060	364,814	990,246
Size of operation (persons engaged)			
1-4 persons	760,706	177,364	583,342
5-9	292,638	92,194	200,444
10-19	177,270	53,546	123,724
20-29	55,114	17,221	37,893
30-49	32,380	11,856	20,524
50-99	19,112	6,592	12,520
100 and over	9,367	3,644	5,723
Loaned or dispatched employees only	8,473	2,397	6,076
Persons engaged	11,843,869	4,003,909	7,839,960
Regular employees	10,226,010	3,532,625	6,693,385
Full-time employees	5,375,398	2,891,265	2,484,133
Other than full-time employees [1]	4,850,612	641,360	4,209,252
Temporary employees	247,780	62,263	185,517
Loaned or dispatched employees from			
the separately operated establishments	366,511	144,921	221,590
Loaned or dispatched employees to			
the separately operated establishments	102,266	79,829	22,437

1) Among regular employees, excludes workers generally referred to as "full-time employees" and "regular members of staff" and includes those referred to as "contract employees", "non-regular members of staff", "part-timers", and similar appellations.

Source: Statistics Bureau, MIC; Ministry of Economy, Trade and Industry.

The number of persons engaged in the wholesale sector was 4 million in 2016, 703,623 of which were persons other than full-time employees (including those who are referred to as "contract employees", "non-regular members of staff", "part-timers", and similar appellations) and temporary employees, making up 17.6 percent of the total.

(2) Retail Trade

The number of retail establishments in operation totaled 990,246 in 2016. Observed by size of operation in terms of persons engaged, establishments with less than 10 persons accounted for 79.2 percent of the total. By type of corporate form, 60.6 percent of them were corporations, while 39.2 percent were individual proprietorships. The proportion of individual proprietorships was higher than that in the wholesale sector.

The number of persons engaged in retail was 7.84 million in 2016, 4.39 million of which were persons other than full-time employees (including those referred to as "contract employees", "non-regular members of staff", "part-timers", and similar appellations) and temporary employees, comprising 56.1 percent of the total.

2. Eating and Drinking Places

There were 590,847 eating and drinking places establishments in operation and 4.12 million persons engaged at them in 2016.

Table 10.2
Eating and Drinking Places (2016)

Size of operation (persons engaged)	Establishments		Persons engaged	
	Number	Ratio (%)	Number	Ratio (%)
Total	590,847	100.0	4,120,279	100.0
1-4 persons	357,056	60.4	767,493	18.6
5-9	114,499	19.4	746,638	18.1
10-19	69,512	11.8	945,207	22.9
20-29	27,877	4.7	662,134	16.1
30 and over	21,025	3.6	998,807	24.2
Loaned or dispatched employees only ..	878	0.1	-	-

Source: Statistics Bureau, MIC; Ministry of Economy, Trade and Industry.

Chapter 11

Trade, International Balance of Payments, and International Cooperation

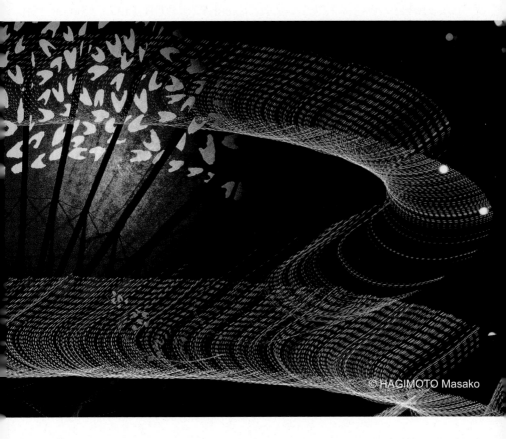

© HAGIMOTO Masako

Japan's official development assistance (ODA) commenced with participation in the Colombo Plan on October 6, 1954.

October 6, the date Japan joined the Colombo Plan, has been established as "International Cooperation Day", with events relating to international cooperation held all over Japan.

1. Trade

(1) Overview of Trade

In 2020, Japan's international trade on a customs clearance basis decreased dramatically, both exports and imports, due to factors such as the worldwide COVID-19 pandemic. Exports (in FOB value) amounted to 68.4 trillion yen, which was a 11.1 percent decrease as compared to the previous year, and a decrease for the second consecutive year. Imports (in CIF value) amounted to 68.0 trillion yen, which was a 13.5 percent decrease as compared to the previous year, and a decrease for the second consecutive year. Trade balance totaled 0.4 trillion yen. This was the trade surplus for the first time in 3 years.

Figure 11.1
Foreign Trade

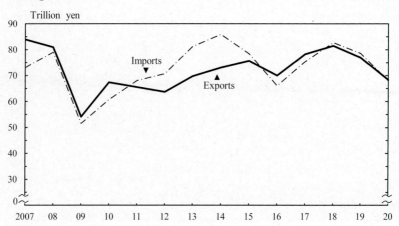

Source: Ministry of Finance.

Table 11.1

Trends in Foreign Trade and Indices of Trade

Year	Value (billion yen) (Customs clearance basis)			Indices of trade (2015=100)					
				Exports			Imports		
	Exports (FOB)	Imports (CIF)	Balance	Value index	Quantum index [1]	Unit value index	Value index	Quantum index [1]	Unit value index
2011	65,546	68,111	-2,565	86.7	107.2	80.9	86.9	99.6	87.2
2012	63,748	70,689	-6,941	84.3	102.0	82.7	90.2	102.0	88.4
2013	69,774	81,243	-11,468	92.3	100.5	91.8	103.6	102.3	101.3
2014	73,093	85,909	-12,816	96.7	101.1	95.7	109.6	102.9	106.5
2015	75,614	78,406	-2,792	100.0	100.0	100.0	100.0	100.0	100.0
2016	70,036	66,042	3,994	92.6	100.5	92.2	84.2	98.8	85.3
2017	78,286	75,379	2,907	103.5	105.9	97.8	96.1	102.9	93.4
2018	81,479	82,703	-1,225	107.8	107.7	100.1	105.5	105.8	99.7
2019	76,932	78,600	-1,668	101.7	103.0	98.8	100.2	104.6	95.9
2020	68,399	68,011	388	90.5	91.0	99.4	86.7	97.9	88.6

1) Quantum index = Value index / Unit value index × 100
Source: Ministry of Finance.

With regard to unit value index, Japan's 2020 exports increased by 0.7 percent from the previous year (the first increase in 2 years), and quantum index decreased by 11.7 percent from the previous year (a decrease for the second consecutive year).

With regard to Japan's imports in 2020, unit value index and quantum index, decreased by 7.5 percent and 6.4 percent compared to the previous year; both indices recorded their second consecutive year of decrease.

(2) Trade by Commodity

As for Japan's exports in 2020 by commodity, transport equipment accounted for the largest portion of the total export value, 21.1 percent, followed by general machinery and electrical machinery, making up 19.2 percent and 18.9 percent, respectively. Motor vehicles, which are in the transport equipment category, constituted 14.0 percent of the total export value, down 20.7 percent in quantity and down 20.0 percent in value from the previous year. One characteristic of Japan's exports is the large proportion of high value-added products manufactured with advanced technology, such as motor vehicles, iron and steel products, and semiconductors, etc.

The leading import item category was electrical machinery, which represented 16.7 percent of the total value imported, followed by mineral fuels and chemicals, with 16.5 percent and 11.6 percent, respectively. Telephony, telegraphy, in the electrical machinery category, constituted 4.2 percent of the total import value, up 0.1 percent from the previous year.

Figure 11.2
Component Ratios of Foreign Trade by Commodity (2020)

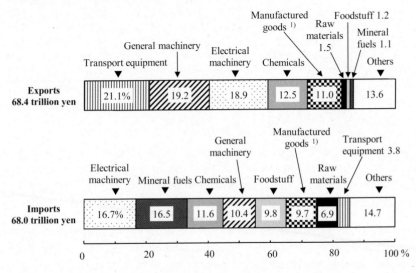

1) Consisting of iron and steel products, nonferrous metals, textile yarn and fabrics, etc.
Source: Ministry of Finance.

Table 11.2
Value of Exports and Imports by Principal Commodity

(Billion yen)

Item	2018	2019	2020	Annual growth (%)
Exports, total	81,479	76,932	68,399	-11.1
Foodstuff	741	754	790	4.8
Raw materials	1,156	1,034	1,020	-1.3
Mineral fuels	1,304	1,383	723	-47.7
Chemicals	8,922	8,739	8,534	-2.4
Plastic materials	2,557	2,430	2,420	-0.4
Manufactured goods [1]	9,136	8,407	7,504	-10.7
Iron and steel products	3,441	3,074	2,574	-16.3
General machinery	16,508	15,122	13,140	-13.1
Semicon machinery, etc.	2,729	2,467	2,517	2.0
Electrical machinery	14,142	13,208	12,898	-2.3
Semiconductors, etc.	4,150	4,006	4,155	3.7
Transport equipment	18,877	18,118	14,456	-20.2
Motor vehicles	12,307	11,971	9,580	-20.0
Others	10,694	10,167	9,334	-8.2
Scientific, optical inst	2,314	2,130	1,968	-7.6
Imports, total	82,703	78,600	68,011	-13.5
Foodstuff	7,247	7,192	6,679	-7.1
Meat and meat preparation	1,516	1,540	1,431	-7.1
Raw materials	4,992	4,861	4,682	-3.7
Ore of nonferrous	1,563	1,378	1,505	9.2
Mineral fuels	19,294	16,951	11,254	-33.6
Petroleum	8,906	7,969	4,646	-41.7
Chemicals	8,550	8,163	7,859	-3.7
Medical products	2,962	3,092	3,197	3.4
Manufactured goods [1]	7,459	7,068	6,564	-7.1
Nonferrous metals	2,000	1,750	1,723	-1.5
General machinery	7,950	7,583	7,043	-7.1
Computers and units	2,029	2,211	2,406	8.8
Electrical machinery	12,338	11,992	11,354	-5.3
Telephony, telegraphy	3,087	2,846	2,850	0.1
Transport equipment	3,490	3,561	2,600	-27.0
Motor vehicles	1,428	1,408	1,165	-17.3
Others	11,383	11,229	9,977	-11.2
Clothing and accessories	3,307	3,205	2,724	-15.0

1) Consisting of iron and steel products, nonferrous metals, textile yarn and fabrics, etc.
Source: Ministry of Finance.

Figure 11.3
Component Ratios of the Value of Major Export and Import Commodities by Country/Region (2020)

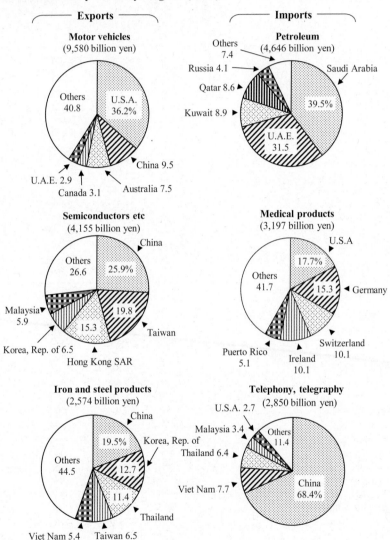

Exports

Motor vehicles
(9,580 billion yen)

Others 40.8
U.S.A. 36.2%
China 9.5
Australia 7.5
Canada 3.1
U.A.E. 2.9

Semiconductors etc
(4,155 billion yen)

Others 26.6
China 25.9%
Taiwan 19.8
Hong Kong SAR 15.3
Korea, Rep. of 6.5
Malaysia 5.9

Iron and steel products
(2,574 billion yen)

Others 44.5
China 19.5%
Korea, Rep. of 12.7
Thailand 11.4
Taiwan 6.5
Viet Nam 5.4

Imports

Petroleum
(4,646 billion yen)

Others 7.4
Russia 4.1
Qatar 8.6
Kuwait 8.9
Saudi Arabia 39.5%
U.A.E. 31.5

Medical products
(3,197 billion yen)

Others 41.7
U.S.A 17.7%
Germany 15.3
Switzerland 10.1
Ireland 10.1
Puerto Rico 5.1

Telephony, telegraphy
(2,850 billion yen)

U.S.A. 2.7
Malaysia 3.4
Thailand 6.4
Viet Nam 7.7
Others 11.4
China 68.4%

Source: Ministry of Finance.

(3) Trade by Country/Region

Japan has maintained a trade surplus with Asia and the U.S.A., while having a continuous trade deficit with the Middle East and Oceania.

Table 11.3
Trends in Value of Exports and Imports by Country/Region

(Billion yen)

Year	Total	Asia	China	Korea, Rep. of	Taiwan	U.S.A.	EU [1]	Middle East	Oceania
Exports from Japan									
2016	70,036	37,107	12,361	5,020	4,268	14,143	7,982	2,585	2,010
2017	78,286	42,920	14,890	5,975	4,558	15,113	8,657	2,350	2,301
2018	81,479	44,736	15,898	5,793	4,679	15,470	9,209	2,434	2,402
2019	76,932	41,327	14,682	5,044	4,689	15,255	8,955	2,356	2,053
2020	68,399	39,220	15,082	4,767	4,739	12,611	6,460	1,809	1,688
Imports to Japan									
2016	66,042	33,199	17,019	2,722	2,495	7,322	8,152	6,501	3,843
2017	75,379	37,026	18,459	3,153	2,848	8,090	8,757	8,243	4,969
2018	82,703	39,218	19,194	3,550	2,998	9,015	9,718	10,375	5,659
2019	78,600	37,413	18,454	3,227	2,928	8,640	9,722	8,852	5,587
2020	68,011	34,678	17,508	2,842	2,863	7,454	7,832	5,558	4,359

1) 28 countries: from July 2013 to Jan. 2020, 27 countries: from Feb. 2020 onward.
Source: Ministry of Finance.

(A) Trade with Asia

Japan's 2020 trade balance with Asia resulted in a 4.5 trillion yen in surplus, an increase for the first time in 3 years (up 16.1 percent from the previous year). Exports (in FOB value) totaled 39.2 trillion yen (down 5.1 percent), a decrease for the second consecutive year; this was mainly due to the contributions for the decrease in transport equipment and general machinery. Imports (in CIF value) amounted to 34.7 trillion yen (down 7.3 percent), a decrease for the second consecutive year; this was mainly contributed to the decrease in mineral fuels and electrical machinery.

In 2020, Japan's trade with China amounted to 15.1 trillion yen in exports and 17.5 trillion yen in imports. The percentage of the total amount of Japan's imports and exports that is accounted for by imports and exports between Japan and China is approximately 20 percent, signifying that China is Japan's largest trading counterpart.

(B) Trade with U.S.A.

Japan's 2020 trade balance with the U.S.A. showed a surplus of 5.2 trillion yen (down 22.0 percent from the previous year), a decrease for the first time in 2 years. Exports (in FOB value) totaled 12.6 trillion yen (down 17.3 percent), a decrease for the second consecutive year. The drop was due mainly to the contributions of transport equipment and general machinery. Imports (in CIF value) totaled 7.5 trillion yen (down 13.7 percent), a decrease for the second consecutive year. The drop was due mainly to the contributions of mineral fuels and transport equipment.

(C) Trade with EU

Japan's 2020 trade balance with the EU (27 countries) registered a deficit of 1.4 trillion yen. Exports (in FOB value) to the EU (27 countries) decreased by 14.6 percent year-on-year, to 6.5 trillion yen. Commodities such as transport equipment and general machinery contributed to the drop in exports. Imports (in CIF value) from the EU (27 countries) totaled 7.8 trillion yen, down 12.1 percent from the previous year. Commodities such as transport equipment and general machinery contributed to the drop in imports.

Figure 11.4
Trends in Value of Exports and Imports by Country/Region

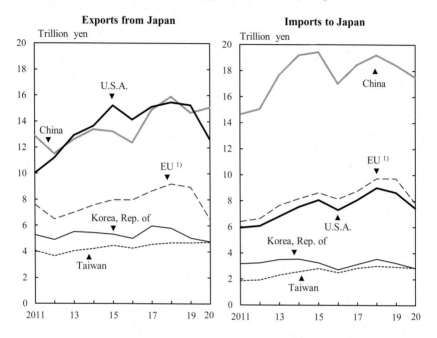

1) 27 countries: from Jan. 2007 to June 2013, 28 countries: from July 2013 to Jan. 2020, 27
countries: from Feb. 2020 onward.
Source: Ministry of Finance.

2. International Balance of Payments

The current account in 2021 totaled 15.5 trillion yen, and its surplus shrank for the fourth consecutive year, due to the trade balance reducing the surplus, etc. Breaking down the current account, goods and services fell by 1.7 trillion yen from the previous year to -2.5 trillion yen, recording a deficit for the third consecutive year. Primary income amounted to 20.5 trillion yen, which was a 7.1 percent increase in its surplus from the previous year.

The financial account amounted to 10.8 trillion yen in 2021, due to factors such as an increase in net assets for direct investment, etc.

Table 11.4
International Balance of Payments

(Billion yen)

Item	2018	2019	2020	2021
Current account	19,504.7	19,251.3	15,673.9	15,487.7
Goods and services	105.2	-931.8	-877.3	-2,561.5
Goods	1,126.5	150.3	2,777.9	1,670.1
Exports	81,226.3	75,775.3	67,262.9	82,283.7
Imports	80,099.8	75,625.0	64,485.1	80,613.6
Services	-1,021.3	-1,082.1	-3,655.2	-4,231.6
Primary income	21,402.6	21,553.1	19,120.9	20,478.1
Secondary income	-2,003.1	-1,370.0	-2,569.7	-2,428.9
Capital account	-210.5	-413.1	-207.2	-419.7
Financial account [1]	20,136.1	24,862.4	13,807.3	10,752.7
Direct investment	14,909.3	23,859.1	9,072.0	13,404.3
Portfolio investment	10,052.8	9,366.6	4,391.6	-22,023.4
Financial derivatives (other than reserves)	123.9	370.0	799.9	2,414.1
Other investment	-7,612.7	-11,537.2	-1,654.1	10,067.7
Reserve assets	2,662.8	2,803.9	1,198.0	6,889.9
Net errors and omissions	841.9	6,024.2	-1,659.4	-4,315.3

1) Positive figures (+) show increase in net assets, negative figures (-) show decrease in net assets.
Source: Ministry of Finance.

Japan's external assets (overseas assets held by residents in Japan) as of the end of 2021 amounted to 1,249.9 trillion yen, while its external liabilities (assets held in Japan by nonresidents) were 838.7 trillion yen. As a result, Japan's net international investment position (external assets minus external liabilities) were 411.2 trillion yen.

Table 11.5

Trends in Japan's International Investment Position [1]

(Billion yen)

Item	2017	2018	2019	2020	2021
Assets	1,013,364	1,018,047	1,090,549	1,144,628	1,249,879
Liabilities	684,062	676,597	733,534	789,597	838,695
Net assets	329,302	341,450	357,015	355,031	411,184

1) End of year.
Source: Ministry of Finance.

Japan's reserve assets remained at around 220 billion U.S. dollars during the period from 1996 to 1998. Beginning in 1999, reserve assets increased continuously. A downward trend started at the end of 2012, but the end of 2017, they began to increase again, and amounted to 1,405.8 billion U.S. dollars (up 0.8 percent) at the end of 2021, marking the fifth consecutive annual increase.

Table 11.6

Reserve Assets

(Million U.S. dollars)

End of year	Total	Foreign currency reserves [1]	IMF reserve position	SDRs	Gold [2]	Other reserve assets [3]
2017	1,264,283	1,202,071	10,582	19,195	31,897	538
2018	1,270,975	1,208,958	11,464	18,484	31,531	538
2019	1,323,750	1,255,322	11,202	19,176	37,469	581
2020	1,394,680	1,312,160	15,147	20,215	46,526	632
2021	1,405,750	1,278,925	10,643	62,330	49,505	4,347

1) Including securities in market value. 2) Market value. 3) Including Asian Bond Fund 2.
Source: Ministry of Finance.

The yen began appreciating sharply in late 2008. From 2011 into 2012, the exchange rate of yen to the U.S. dollar stayed between the higher 70 yen range and the lower 80 yen range. In April 2013, the Bank of Japan introduced Quantitative and Qualitative Monetary Easing (QQME) to put an end to deflation. Based on this, the exchange rate shifted towards yen depreciation. Subsequently, the yen strengthened from early to mid 2016, followed by a leveling off phase from 2017. However, from March 2022, there was a general appreciation of the currencies of resource-producing countries, including the U.S.A., against a backdrop of higher resource prices. Awareness of the different directions of monetary policy in Japan and the U.S.A., and factors such as dollar buying by Japanese importing firms, have led to a weakening yen-dollar exchange rate. As of April 2022, the exchange rate was 130.6 yen per U.S. dollar.

Figure 11.5
Yen Exchange Rate against the U.S. Dollar

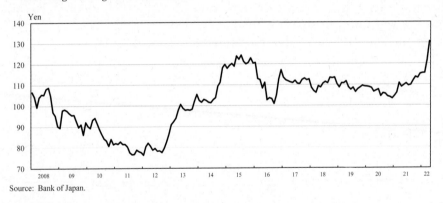

Source: Bank of Japan.

3. International Cooperation

In Japan, there are diverse international cooperation donors: Official Development Assistance (ODA) by the government, direct investments and export credits by private corporations, grants by private non-profit organizations, assistance activities by NGOs and volunteer citizen groups, etc. With regard to ODA, there are various forms, including bilateral assistance, which assists developing countries and regions directly, and multilateral assistance, which contributes to international organizations.

Table 11.7

Financial Flows to Developing Countries

(Million U.S. dollars)

Item	Net disbursements [1]		Grant equivalent [2]	
	2019	2020	2019	2020
Total value	55,519	32,472	...	...
Official flows	12,033	18,558	...	...
Official Development Assistance (ODA)	11,720	13,660	15,588	16,260
Bilateral official development assistance [3]	7,477	10,242	11,794	13,180
Grants [3]	5,278	5,469	5,278	5,469
Grant assistance [3]	2,556	3,067	2,556	3,067
Technical assistance	2,722	2,401	2,722	2,401
Loans	2,199	4,774	6,516	7,712
Contributions to multilateral institutions	4,243	3,418	3,794	3,080
Other Official Flows (OOF)	313	4,898	...	...
Export credits (over 1 year)	755	3	...	...
Direct investment and others	-443	4,895	...	...
Contributions to multilateral institutions	-	-	-	-
Private Flows (PF)	42,913	13,309	...	...
Export credits (over 1 year)	-2,112	-5,414	...	...
Direct investment	39,067	25,031	...	...
Other bilateral securities and claims	5,770	-4,213	...	...
Contributions to multilateral institutions	188	-2,095	...	...
Grants by private non-profit organizations	574	606	...	...
ODA as percentage of GNI (%)	0.22	0.26	0.29	0.31
ODA as percentage of GNI (DAC average) (%)	...	...	0.30	0.33

1) Net disbursements at current prices and exchange rate designated by DAC. Negative figures (-) indicate that loan repayments, etc., exceeded the disbursed amount. 2) Grant equivalent at current prices and exchange rate designated by DAC. 3) Including bilateral grants through multilateral institutions.
Source: Ministry of Foreign Affairs; Ministry of Finance; OECD.

In the ODA framework, Japan's spending (on a grant equivalent basis at current prices) in 2020 was increased by 4.3 percent over the previous year to 16.3 billion U.S. dollars. Japan contributed to the growth of developing countries as the world's number-one ODA donor for 10 consecutive years up until 2000. Recently, Japan's ODA budget has been levelling off because of the country's severe fiscal situation.

With regard to the comparison of the ODA grant equivalents in 2020 of the member countries of the Development Assistance Committee (DAC) of the OECD, Japan was the fourth-largest contributor behind the U.S.A., Germany and the U.K. The ratio of Japan's ODA grant equivalent to Gross National Income (GNI) was 0.31 percent, or an increase of 0.02 percentage points compared with that of the previous year.

Figure 11.6
Trends in ODA by Country [1)]

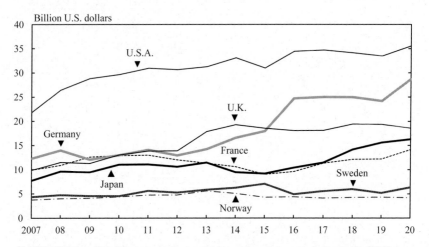

1) 2007-2017 data: Net disbursement at current prices and exchange rate designated by DAC.
2018-2020 data: Grant equivalent at current prices and exchange rate designated by DAC.
Source: OECD.

Of the 16.3 billion U.S. dollars in ODA grant equivalent provided by Japan in 2020, 13.2 billion was bilateral ODA (up 11.8 percent year-on-year), and 3.1 billion was ODA contributed through multilateral institutions (down 18.8 percent).

Bilateral ODA (grant equivalent at current prices) provided in 2020 consisted of 3.1 billion U.S. dollars of grant assistance, 2.4 billion of technical assistance, and 7.7 billion of loans.

By region, bilateral ODA (net disbursement at current prices, including assistance to graduated countries) was distributed as follows: Asia, 4,777 million U.S. dollars; Sub-Saharan Africa, 1,207 million U.S. dollars; Middle East and North Africa, 1,151 million U.S. dollars; Latin America and the Caribbean, 391 million U.S. dollars; Oceania, 318 million U.S. dollars; and Europe, 7 million U.S. dollars.

Table 11.8

Regional Distribution of Bilateral ODA [1] (2020)

(Million U.S. dollars)

Region	Net disbursements
Total	10,216
Asia	4,777
ASEAN	1,948
Middle East and North Africa	1,151
Sub-Saharan Africa	1,207
Latin America and the Caribbean	391
Oceania	318
Europe	7
Multiple regions, etc.	2,365

1) Net disbursement at current prices and exchange rate
designated by DAC. Including assistance to graduated
countries. The negative figure (-) indicates that repayments
of loans, etc. exceeded the disbursed amount.
Source: Ministry of Foreign Affairs.

Bilateral ODA in 2020 (including assistance to graduated countries) was broken down by purpose (on a commitments basis) as follows: 42.1 percent for improving "economic infrastructure and services" (including transport, storage and energy), followed in descending order by "social infrastructure and services", at 23.3 percent.

Figure 11.7
Distribution of Bilateral ODA by Sector [1] (2020)

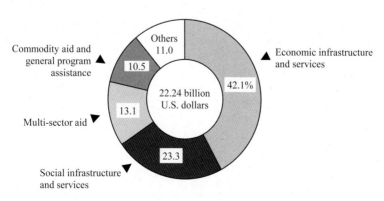

1) Commitments basis. Including assistance to graduated countries.
Source: Ministry of Foreign Affairs.

In addition to the financial assistance described above, Japan has also been active in the areas of human resources development and technology transfer through its ODA activities, both of which are vital to the growth of developing countries.

Table 11.9

Number of Persons Involved in Technical Cooperation by Type [1]

Type of cooperation	FY2015	FY2017	FY2018	FY2019	FY2020
Total	46,771	39,932	34,592	26,607	6,101
Trainees received	25,203	17,138	14,905	12,187	5,290
Dispatched					
Experts	11,134	11,098	9,874	8,012	553
Research team	8,914	10,228	8,584	5,257	238
Japan Overseas					
Cooperation Volunteers	1,198	1,171	1,029	999	10
Other volunteers	322	297	200	152	10

1) Numbers of persons newly received/dispatched in the aforementioned fiscal year.
Source: Japan International Cooperation Agency.

Chapter 12

Labour

Marunouchi Naka-dori is the main street of Marunouchi, running from Harumi-dori Avenue near Hibiya Station to Gyoko-dori Avenue in front of Tokyo Station. The street is lined with office buildings, commercial facilities, restaurants, cafes, and other amenities.

1. Labour Force

After the population in Japan aged 15 years old and over peaked at 111.18 million people in 2017, it has been broadly flat since 2018. In 2021, this population reached 110.87 million people.

In the 2000s, the labour force (among the population aged 15 years old and over, the total of employed persons and unemployed persons) had been on a downward trend due to the aging of the population, but began to increase in 2013 and continued to increase until 2019. In 2020, there was a decrease due to the effects of COVID-19, but in 2021, the figure was 69.07 million, an increase of 0.05 million (0.1 percent) from the previous year and the first increase in 2 years.

The labour force participation rate (the rate of the labour force to the population aged 15 years old and over) was 62.1 percent in 2021 (up 0.1 percentage points from the previous year). Observed by gender, the rate was 71.3 percent for males (down 0.1 percentage points) and 53.5 percent for females (up 0.3 percentage points).

Table 12.1
Population by Labour Force Status

(Thousands)

Year	Population aged 15 years old and over	Labour force			Not in labour force	Unemploy- ment rate (%)
		Total	Employed	Unemployed		
Total						
2005	110,080	66,510	63,560	2,940	43,460	4.4
2010	111,110	66,320	62,980	3,340	44,730	5.1
2015	111,100	66,250	64,020	2,220	44,790	3.4
2018	111,160	68,490	66,820	1,670	42,580	2.4
2019	111,120	69,120	67,500	1,620	41,910	2.4
2020	111,080	69,020	67,100	1,920	41,970	2.8
2021	110,870	69,070	67,130	1,950	41,710	2.8
Males						
2005	53,230	39,010	37,230	1,780	14,160	4.6
2010	53,650	38,500	36,430	2,070	15,130	5.4
2015	53,650	37,730	36,390	1,350	15,880	3.6
2018	53,670	38,260	37,260	990	15,370	2.6
2019	53,660	38,410	37,440	960	15,200	2.5
2020	53,640	38,400	37,240	1,150	15,200	3.0
2021	53,510	38,270	37,110	1,170	15,200	3.1
Females						
2005	56,850	27,500	26,330	1,160	29,300	4.2
2010	57,460	27,830	26,560	1,280	29,600	4.6
2015	57,460	28,520	27,640	890	28,910	3.1
2018	57,490	30,240	29,560	670	27,210	2.2
2019	57,470	30,720	30,050	660	26,700	2.2
2020	57,440	30,630	29,860	760	26,770	2.5
2021	57,350	30,800	30,020	780	26,510	2.5

Source: Statistics Bureau, MIC.

The female labour force participation rate by age group is in an M-shaped curve, which implies that females leave the labour force when they get married or give birth and then rejoin the labour force after their child has grown. However, the shape of the M-shaped curve has been changing in recent years. A comparison with the data from 20 years ago (2001) shows that, in 2021, the 35-39 age group replaced the 30-34 age group to form the bottom of the M-shaped curve. The participation rate rose by 20.6

percentage points in the 30-34 age group and by 15.4 percentage points in the 35-39 age group, making the bottom of the M-shaped curve flatter and more gradual. While this is thought to be greatly affected by the progression of enhancement of the legal system to balance work and childcare, and the improvement of work environment of companies, there are also effects from the trend of getting married and having children later in life.

Figure 12.1
Labour Force Participation Rate by Gender and Age Group

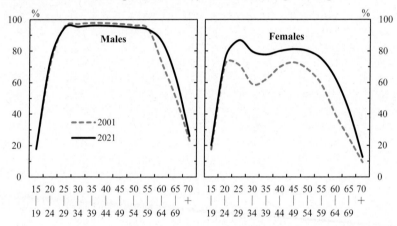

Source: Statistics Bureau, MIC.

2. Employment

The number of employed persons declined between 2008 and 2012, before increasing between 2013 and 2019. The increase amounted to 0.03 million in 2021, from 67.10 million (60.3 percent of the population aged 15 years old and over) in the previous year to 67.13 million (60.4 percent).

(1) Employment by Industry

In 2021, the primary industry accounted for 3.1 percent of the total of employed persons; the secondary industry, 23.2 percent; and the tertiary industry, 73.6 percent.

Figure 12.2
Structure of Employment by Country [1]

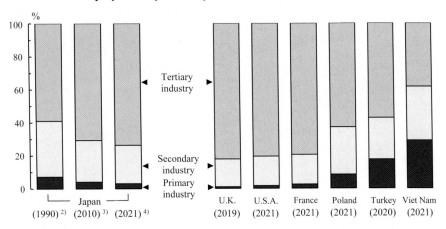

1) As to the countries other than Japan, the industrial classification is the International Standard Industrial Classification of All Economic Activities, Revision 4 (ISIC Rev.4).
2) The industrial classification is the 10th revision of the Japan Standard Industrial Classification (JSIC).
3) The industrial classification is the 12th revision of the JSIC.
4) The industrial classification is the 13th revision of the JSIC.
Source: Statistics Bureau, MIC; International Labour Organization.

Over the long term, the percentage of persons employed in the primary industry and in the secondary industry have been continually falling, while the percentage of persons employed in the tertiary industry has been continually rising. Within the tertiary industry, the number of those in "medical, health care and welfare" has been increasing.

Depending on the industrial sector, a difference was seen in the employment tendency between males and females. In 2021, the percentage of male employment was highest in "construction", followed by "electricity, gas, heat supply and water" and "transport and postal activities". The percentage of female employment was highest in "medical, health care and welfare", followed by "accommodations, eating and drinking services" and "living-related and personal services and amusement services".

Table 12.2
Employment by Industry

(Thousands)

Industries	2018	2019	2020	2021	Percentage [1]	
					Males	Females
Total [2]	66,820	67,500	67,100	67,130	55.3	44.7
Primary industry	**2,280**	**2,220**	**2,130**	**2,080**	**62.5**	**37.5**
Agriculture and forestry	2,100	2,070	2,000	1,950	61.5	38.5
Fisheries	180	150	130	130	76.9	23.1
Secondary industry	**15,720**	**15,700**	**15,470**	**15,330**	**74.1**	**25.9**
Mining and quarrying of stone and gravel	30	20	20	30	66.7	33.3
Construction	5,050	5,000	4,940	4,850	82.9	17.1
Manufacturing	10,640	10,680	10,510	10,450	70.0	30.0
Tertiary industry	**47,460**	**48,080**	**48,260**	**48,660**	**49.1**	**50.9**
Electricity, gas, heat supply and water	280	280	320	340	82.4	17.6
Information and communications	2,210	2,300	2,410	2,580	71.3	28.7
Transport and postal activities	3,420	3,480	3,490	3,520	78.2	21.8
Wholesale and retail trade	10,760	10,640	10,620	10,690	48.2	51.8
Finance and insurance	1,640	1,670	1,670	1,680	44.6	55.4
Real estate and goods rental and leasing	1,300	1,300	1,400	1,420	59.2	40.8
Scientific research, professional and technical services	2,400	2,410	2,450	2,540	63.8	36.2
Accommodations, eating and drinking services	4,170	4,210	3,920	3,710	38.0	62.0
Living-related and personal services and amusement services	2,360	2,420	2,360	2,270	40.3	59.7
Education, learning support	3,220	3,360	3,410	3,480	41.7	58.3
Medical, health care and welfare	8,340	8,470	8,670	8,910	24.7	75.3
Compound services	570	540	510	500	58.8	41.2
Services, N.E.C.	4,460	4,570	4,540	4,520	59.5	40.5
Government [3]	2,330	2,430	2,490	2,500	68.8	31.2

1) Calculated from figures rounded to thousands.
2) Including "Industries unable to classify". 3) Excluding elsewhere classified.
Source: Statistics Bureau, MIC.

Figure 12.3
Distribution of Employment by Industry (2021)

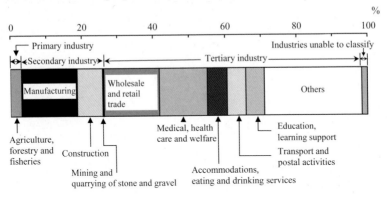

Source: Statistics Bureau, MIC.

(2) Employment by Occupation

In terms of occupation, the "administrative and managerial workers" has been declining in recent years. The number was 1.29 million in 2021, the same as the previous year. In contrast, "service workers" such as home-care workers have been on a rising trend over the past few years due to a trend toward a service-oriented economy, the aging population, and improvements on welfare services. There is also a rising trend in the number of "professional and engineering workers". The number was 12.65 million in 2021, which accounted for approximately 18.8 percent of the total employed persons.

Table 12.3
Employment by Occupation

(Thousands)

Occupation	2018	2019	2020	2021	Percentage	
					Males	Females
Total [1]	66,820	67,500	67,100	67,130	55.3	44.7
Administrative and managerial workers	1,350	1,290	1,290	1,290	86.8	13.2
Professional and engineering workers	11,350	11,790	12,210	12,650	52.0	48.0
Clerical workers	13,160	13,260	13,600	13,890	39.8	60.2
Sales workers	8,660	8,590	8,520	8,480	55.7	44.3
Service workers	8,460	8,520	8,310	8,060	31.5	68.5
Security workers	1,310	1,330	1,330	1,300	92.2	7.8
Agricultural, forestry and fishery workers	2,220	2,170	2,090	2,030	64.5	35.5
Manufacturing process workers	9,140	9,110	8,730	8,650	70.3	29.7
Transport and machine operation workers	2,190	2,220	2,180	2,140	96.7	3.3
Construction and mining workers	2,990	2,940	2,930	2,840	97.5	2.5
Carrying, cleaning, packaging, and related workers	4,770	4,920	4,820	4,880	55.3	44.7

1) Including figures unclassifiable or not reported.
Source: Statistics Bureau, MIC.

In 2021, the percentages of male and female employed persons by occupation show that males were particularly prominent among "construction and mining workers" (97.5 percent) and "transport and machine operation workers" (96.7 percent). Females were prominent among "service workers" (68.5 percent) and "clerical workers" (60.2 percent).

(3) Employment by Employment Pattern

With regard to the trends in the number of employed persons by employment pattern, the number of non-regular staff members (such as part-time workers and agency-dispatched workers) has been increasing continuously for 10 consecutive years since 2010. However, in 2020, it decreased for the first time in 11 years, and in 2021 it decreased again for the second consecutive year. The number of regular staff members was on a slight declining trend in the 2000s and the early 2010s, but began to rise in 2015 and has continued to rise for 7 years in a row.

In 2021, there were 56.62 million employees (excluding company executives), 20.75 million of whom, or 36.7 percent, were non-regular staff members. The ratio of non-regular staff members among all male employees was 21.8 percent, while the corresponding ratio for females was 53.6 percent, revealing a large difference between the genders.

With regard to the percentage of non-regular staff members to the total of regular and non-regular staff members by gender and age group, for males, the percentages of young people aged 15 to 24 years old, and the elderly aged 65 years old and over were high. Among females, non-regular staff members accounted for more than 50 percent across all age groups, with the exception of females aged 25 to 34 and 35 to 44 years old.

Table 12.4
Employment by Employment Pattern (2021)

(Thousands)

	Employees [1)	Regular staff members	Percentage	Non-regular staff members	Percentage
Total	56,620	35,870	63.3	20,750	36.7
Males	30,070	23,530	78.2	6,530	21.8
Females	26,550	12,330	46.4	14,220	53.6

1) Excluding company executives.
Source: Statistics Bureau, MIC.

Figure 12.4
Employment Pattern by Gender and Age Group (2021)

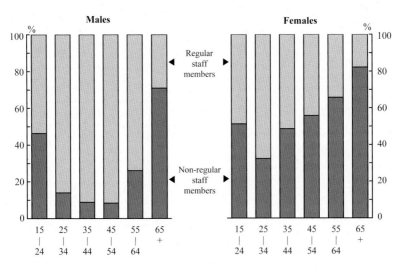

Source: Statistics Bureau, MIC.

131

With regard to the main reasons for the current employment patterns of males and females who are non-regular staff members, for males, the reason "For working at convenient times" was the most popular, on average in 2021, with 1.87 million males (30.2 percent) choosing this reason, up 0.01 million people as compared to the previous year. The most popular reason among females was also "For working at convenient times", with 4.70 million females (34.0 percent) choosing this reason, up 0.34 million people.

The employment rate of new graduates was not good as a result of the economic slowdown since 2008, but in recent years, their employment situation has been on an improving trend.

3. Unemployment

In 2021, the number of unemployed persons stood at 1.95 million people, up 1.6 percent from the previous year, an increase for the second consecutive year. The unemployment rate was 2.8 percent, the same as the previous year.

The active job openings-to-applicants ratio had been on an upward trend from 2009 to 2019. However, as a result of the impact of COVID-19, the ratio began to decline in 2020, and in 2021 it stood at 1.13 times, down 0.05 points from the previous year.

Figure 12.5
Unemployment Rate and Active Job Openings-to-Applicants Ratio

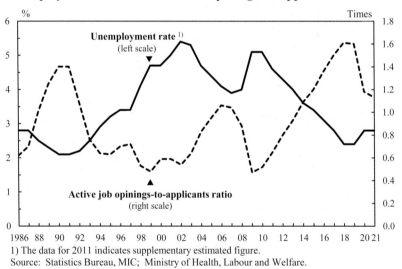

1) The data for 2011 indicates supplementary estimated figure.
Source: Statistics Bureau, MIC; Ministry of Health, Labour and Welfare.

The breakdown by gender shows that the unemployment rate in 2021 was 3.1 percent among males, and 2.5 percent among females. The unemployment rate among males has been higher since 1998.

The unemployment rate was higher in younger age groups than in other age groups, in males and females alike.

Figure 12.6
Unemployment Rates by Gender and Age Group (2021)

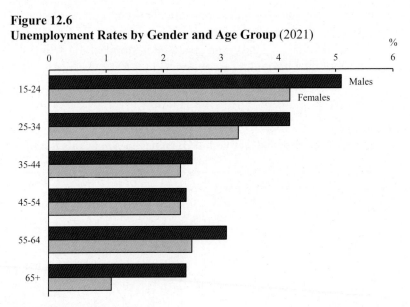

Source: Statistics Bureau, MIC.

With regard to the total number of unemployed persons in 2021, by reason for job-seeking, the major reasons were: (i) involuntary separation due to corporate or business circumstances, or reaching retirement age limit, 0.56 million persons; (ii) voluntary separation for personal or family reasons, 0.74 million persons; (iii) new job seekers due to the necessity to earn income, 0.26 million; and (iv) new job seekers just graduated from school, 0.07 million.

In terms of the duration of unemployment, the largest was unemployed for "1 year or more" (0.67 million persons), followed by "less than 3 months" (0.66 million persons).

Figure 12.7
Unemployment Rates by Country

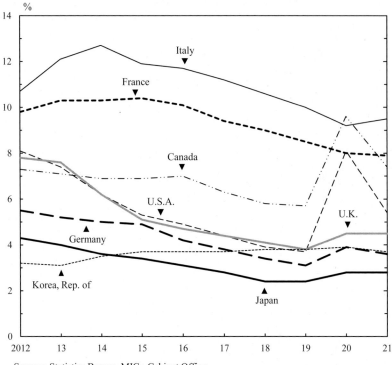

Source: Statistics Bureau, MIC; Cabinet Office.

4. Hours Worked and Cash Earnings

In 2021, the monthly average of total hours worked was 136.1 per regular employee (in establishments with 5 or more regular employees), up 0.6 percent from the previous year, and an annual average was 1,633 hours.

Of the total monthly hours worked per regular employee, 126.4 were scheduled hours worked, representing an increase of 0.4 percent from the previous year. Non-scheduled hours worked such as overtime work were 9.7 hours, representing an increase of 5.1 percent from the previous year. Monthly days worked per regular employee were 17.7 days in 2021.

In 2021, the monthly average of total cash earnings per regular employee (in establishments with 5 or more regular employees) was 319,461 yen. This total amount consists of 263,739 yen in "contractual cash earnings" (total for "scheduled cash earnings" and "non-scheduled cash earnings" for working overtime, on holidays and late at night, as well as other allowances), and 55,722 yen in "special cash earnings" (which include summer and year-end bonuses, payments to celebrate employees' marriages, etc.).

Table 12.5
Hours Worked and Cash Earnings [1] (Monthly average)

Year	Days worked	Hours Worked			Cash Earnings (1,000 yen)				
		Total	Scheduled	Non-scheduled	Total	Contractual	Scheduled	Non-scheduled	Special [2]
2017	18.5	143.3	132.4	10.9	319	262	243	20	57
2018	18.4	142.2	131.4	10.8	324	265	245	20	59
2019	18.0	139.1	128.5	10.6	323	264	244	20	58
2020	17.7	135.1	125.9	9.2	318	262	245	17	56
2021	17.7	136.1	126.4	9.7	319	264	246	18	56
Indices (2015 average = 100)									
2017	-	99.3	99.2	99.6	101.1	100.7	100.8	-	-
2018	-	98.5	98.4	98.1	102.5	101.6	101.6	-	-
2019	-	96.3	96.2	96.2	102.1	101.4	101.5	-	-
2020	-	93.6	94.3	83.5	100.9	100.7	101.7	-	-
2021	-	94.2	94.7	87.8	101.2	101.2	102.0	-	-

1) Establishments with 5 or more regular employees.
2) Bonuses and other special allowances.
Source: Ministry of Health, Labour and Welfare.

The average earnings (scheduled cash earnings) in Japan go up with age until roughly the 40s to mid-50s and then decline. In revising salaries, about half of all companies emphasize "corporate performance", but in the context of worsening labour shortages, a rising percentage of companies in recent years have been placing the greatest emphasis on "securing and retaining their labour force".

Figure 12.8
Monthly Scheduled Cash Earnings by Size of Enterprise, Gender, and Age Group (2021)

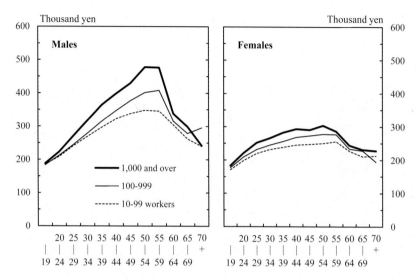

Source: Ministry of Health, Labour and Welfare.

Chapter 13

Family Budgets and Prices

© IMAI Hideyuki

A twilight scene. December is a time with many events, including year-end parties, Christmas, and New Year's Eve. People are doing things like preparing for New Year's Day, and this is the month with the highest consumer spending of the year.

1. Family Budgets

In 2020, there were approximately 56 million private households in Japan, of which about 62 percent are two-or-more-person households and about 38 percent are one-person households. Family budgets vary significantly depending on the employment situation and ages of their members. In this section, family budgets in various types of households are described on the basis of the 2021 results of the "Family Income and Expenditure Survey".

(1) Income and Expenditure

(A) Two-or-more-person Households

The 2021 average monthly consumption expenditures per two-or-more-person household (the average number of household members being 2.93 and the average age of the household head being 60.1 years) was 279,024 yen. Compared to the previous year, it increased by 0.4 percent in nominal terms and increased by 0.7 percent in real terms. The share of food expenses to total consumption expenditures (Engel's coefficient) was 27.2 percent.

Results for 2021 marked the first increase, in the 2 years since 2019, in the real annual change rate in consumption expenditures.

Figure 13.1
Average Monthly Consumption Expenditures per Household [1]
(Two-or-more-person households) (2021)

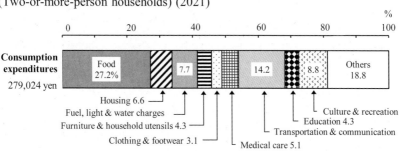

1) Use Classification.
Source: Statistics Bureau, MIC.

(a) Workers' Households

A workers' household means a household of which the head is employed by a company, public office, school, factory, store, etc. The average income of workers' households (the average number of household members being 3.28 and the average age of the household head being 50.1 years) was 605,316 yen in 2021. With regard to the breakdown of income, regular income by the household head makes up the majority. The ratio of income by spouses has been increasing little by little, however.

Table 13.1

Average Monthly Income and Expenditures per Household (Workers' households [1])

(Thousand yen)

Item	2017	2018	2019	2020	2021
Income (A)	533.8	558.7	586.1	609.5	605.3
Wages and salaries	493.8	512.6	536.3	536.9	551.0
Others	40.0	46.1	49.8	72.7	54.3
Disposable income (A-C)	434.4	455.1	476.6	498.6	492.7
Expenditures	412.5	418.9	433.4	416.7	422.1
Consumption expenditures (B)	313.1	315.3	323.9	305.8	309.5
Non-consumption expenditures (C) [2]	99.4	103.6	109.5	110.9	112.6
Surplus ((A-C)-B)	121.4	139.8	152.8	192.8	183.2
Net increase in deposits and insurance	97.0	121.1	149.7	175.5	168.7
Average propensity to consume (%) [3]	72.1	69.3	67.9	61.3	62.8
Ratio of net increase in deposits and insurance (%) [4]	22.3	26.6	31.4	35.2	34.2
Engel's coefficient (%)	23.8	24.1	23.9	26.0	25.4
Annual change (%) (real terms)					
Disposable income	0.7	3.6	4.1	4.6	-0.9
Consumption expenditures	0.5	-0.5	2.1	-5.6	1.5

1) Two-or-more-person households. 2) Direct taxes, social insurance contributions, etc. 3) Ratio of consumption expenditures to disposable income. 4) Ratio of net increase in deposits and insurance to disposable income.
Source: Statistics Bureau, MIC.

Disposable income, calculated as income minus non-consumption expenditures such as taxes and social insurance contributions, was 492,681 yen. Of this disposable income, 309,469 yen was used for living expenses (consumption expenditures), such as food and housing expenses, while the remainder (surplus), totaling 183,213 yen, was applied to savings, life insurance premiums and repaying debts such as housing loans.

Figure 13.2
Balance of Income and Expenditures
(Monthly average per household, workers' households [1]) (2021)

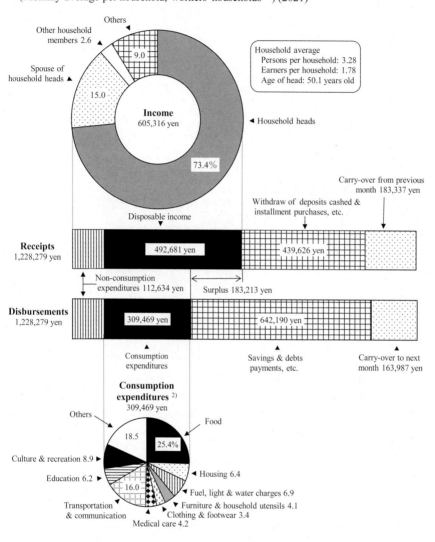

1) Two-or-more-person households. 2) Use Classification.
Source: Statistics Bureau, MIC.

141

A comparison of consumption expenditures by category showed that spending on "education" and "transportation and communication", etc. increased from the previous year in real terms, while spending on "furniture and household utensils" and "food", etc. decreased in real terms.

Figure 13.3
Year-on-Year Change in Average Monthly Income and Consumption Expenditures per Household (Workers' households [1])

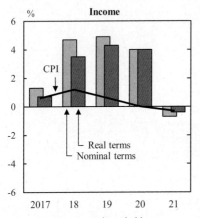 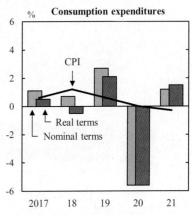

1) Two-or-more-person households.
Source: Statistics Bureau, MIC.

Family budgets differ among households according to their stages in life. Observed by age group of the household head, the 2021 average monthly disposable income of workers' households was the highest in households in the 50s group (548,100 yen), followed by those in the 40s group (527,972 yen) and the 30s group (476,698 yen).

The 2021 average propensity to consume (the ratio of consumption expenditures to disposable income) was the lowest in households in the under 29 group (54.2 percent). The figure was 55.7 percent for households in the 30s group, 59.8 percent in the 40s group, 63.5 percent in the 50s group, 74.9 percent in the 60s group, and 72.5 percent in the 70 and over group. The percentage tends to be higher as the age goes up, except for the 70 and over group. Meanwhile, a net increase in financial assets (an amount added to savings) was the highest in households in the 50s group, followed by those in the 40s group.

Figure 13.4
Average Monthly Family Income and Consumption Expenditures per Household by Age Group of Household Head
(Workers' households [1]) (2021)

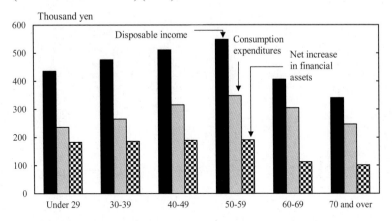

1) Two-or-more-person households.
Source: Statistics Bureau, MIC.

(b) Non-working Elderly Households

According to an analysis of the average monthly income and expenditures of non-working elderly households (two-or-more-person households where the age of the household head is 60 and over), the average income was 245,316 yen in 2021. Social security benefits amounted to 197,097 yen, thus accounting for 80.3 percent of income.

Disposable income averaged 212,553 yen, while consumption expenditures averaged 229,456 yen. The average propensity to consume in non-working elderly households was 108.0 percent, which means consumption expenditures exceeded disposable income. The deficit of disposable income to consumption expenditures (16,903 yen) increased from that of the previous year (1,200 yen). This deficit was financed by withdrawing financial assets such as deposits, etc.

Figure 13.5
Average Monthly Income and Expenditures per Household [1)] [2)]
(Non-working elderly households [3)]) (2021)

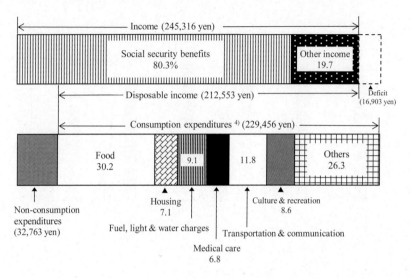

1) The percentage of "Social security benefits" and "Other income" in the graph is in proportion to the income. 2) The percentage from "Food" to "Others" in the graph is in proportion to the consumption expenditures. 3) Two-or-more-person households.
4) Use Classification.
Source: Statistics Bureau, MIC.

(B) One-person Households

The average monthly consumption expenditures of one-person households in 2021 was 155,046 yen, up 3.0 percent in nominal terms and up 3.3 percent in real terms from the previous year. By age group, the average monthly consumption expenditures was 157,411 yen for the under 34 group, 180,109 yen for the 35-59 age group, and 141,126 yen for the 60 and over group. Spending on categories such as "food", "fuel, light and water charges" and "medical care" tended to be larger in older age groups. On the other hand, expenditures on "housing" and "clothing and footwear" decreased in each successively older age groups.

Table 13.2

Average Monthly Consumption Expenditures per Household by Age Group
(One-person households) (2021)

(Yen)

Item	Average Actual figures	Average ratio (%)	Under 34 Actual figures	Under 34 ratio (%)	35-59 Actual figures	35-59 ratio (%)	60 and over Actual figures	60 and over ratio (%)
Consumption expenditures [1] ...	155,046	100.0	157,411	100.0	180,109	100.0	141,126	100.0
Food	38,410	24.8	35,418	22.5	42,108	23.4	37,629	26.7
Housing	22,116	14.3	35,951	22.8	27,842	15.5	13,867	9.8
Fuel, light and water charges	11,383	7.3	7,675	4.9	11,480	6.4	12,747	9.0
Furniture and household utensils	5,687	3.7	6,954	4.4	5,452	3.0	5,320	3.8
Clothing and footwear	4,606	3.0	6,509	4.1	5,096	2.8	3,616	2.6
Medical care	7,625	4.9	4,683	3.0	7,462	4.1	8,832	6.3
Transportation and communication	18,856	12.2	20,152	12.8	25,059	13.9	15,151	10.7
Education	7	0.0	11	0.0	6	0.0	7	0.0
Culture and recreation	17,106	11.0	19,839	12.6	21,329	11.8	13,864	9.8
Others	29,251	18.9	20,220	12.8	34,275	19.0	30,093	21.3
Annual change (%) (real terms) Consumption expenditures	3.3		...		...		...	

1) Use Classification.
Source: Statistics Bureau, MIC.

(2) Savings and Debts

Two-or-more-person households in 2021 showed that the average amount of savings per workers' household was 14.54 million yen, resulting in a ratio to yearly income (7.49 million yen) of 194.1 percent. The median value of household savings (the current household savings of the household exactly in the middle when all households, excluding those with 0 savings, are listed in order from lowest to highest amount of savings) was 8.33 million yen. On the other hand, the average amount of debts per household was 8.56 million yen, which was 114.3 percent relative to yearly income. The median value of households holding debts (the current household debts of the household exactly in the middle when all households, excluding those with 0 debts, are listed in order from lowest to highest amount of debts) was 14.68 million yen. The portion of household debts accounted for by "housing and/or land" averaged 7.91 million yen. A total of 42.4 percent of workers' households held "debts for housing and/or land".

Table 13.3

Average Amount of Savings and Debts (Workers' households [1])

(Thousand yen)

Year	Yearly income	Savings	Ratio of savings to yearly income (%)	Debts	Housing and/or land	Ratio of debts to yearly income (%)	Ratio of households holding debts (%)
2017	7,220	13,270	183.8	7,940	7,390	110.0	54.1
2018	7,290	13,200	181.1	8,210	7,610	112.6	54.6
2019	7,360	13,760	187.0	8,550	7,980	116.2	55.3
2020	7,400	13,780	186.2	8,510	7,910	115.0	54.3
2021	7,490	14,540	194.1	8,560	7,910	114.3	53.4

1) Two-or-more-person households.
Source: Statistics Bureau, MIC.

By age group of household head, the average amount of savings was found to be the highest in the 60s group, while debts were the highest in the 30s group.

Table 13.4

Amount of Savings and Debts by Age Group of Household Head

(Workers' households [1]) (2021)

(Million yen)

Item	Average	Under 29	30-39	40-49	50-59	60-69	70 and over
Yearly income	7.49	5.95	6.66	7.59	8.78	6.75	5.37
Savings	14.54	4.14	7.72	11.34	17.75	22.07	18.83
Financial institutions	14.11	3.97	7.48	10.86	17.09	21.76	18.77
Demand deposits	5.21	2.04	4.10	4.51	5.71	7.13	5.31
Time deposits	3.99	0.61	1.37	2.59	4.86	7.49	6.45
Life insurance, etc.	2.93	0.80	1.24	2.35	3.82	4.25	3.77
Securities	1.98	0.52	0.77	1.41	2.70	2.90	3.24
Non-financial institutions	0.44	0.17	0.24	0.48	0.67	0.31	0.06
Debts	8.56	8.14	14.64	11.79	6.52	2.20	0.77
Housing and/or land	7.91	7.64	13.87	10.92	5.95	1.82	0.60
Other than housing and/or land ...	0.43	0.30	0.61	0.62	0.34	0.15	0.05
Monthly and yearly installments ..	0.22	0.20	0.16	0.25	0.23	0.23	0.13

1) Two-or-more-person households.
Source: Statistics Bureau, MIC.

(3) Internet Shopping by Households

Due to popularization of computers, smartphones, etc., the use of Internet shopping has been increasing. According to the "Survey of Household Economy", the percentage of two-or-more-person households that utilize Internet shopping has continued to increase since 2002, reaching 52.7 percent in 2021. Total monthly expenditures used on Internet shopping amounted to an average of 18,727 yen per household.

Figure 13.6
Proportion of Households Ordered over the Internet
(Two-or-more-person households)

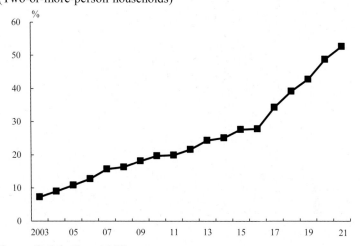

Source: Statistics Bureau, MIC.

Looking at the breakdown of total expenditures per two-or-more-person households spent on Internet shopping, "food" were the highest at 22.5 percent, followed by "clothing and footwear" at 11.8 percent, "home electronics and furniture" at 10.3 percent, "culture-related" (such as books and music software) at 9.4 percent, and "travel-related" at 8.2 percent, etc.

Figure 13.7
Ratio of Expenditure on Goods and Services Ordered over the Internet
(Two-or-more-person households) (2021)

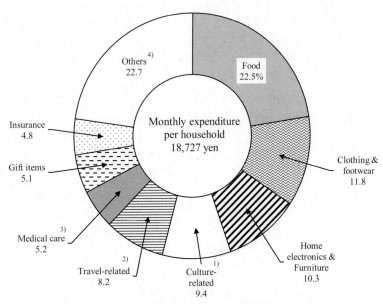

1) Total of books and other reading materials, software (music, video, personal computer, TV game), digital books, download music, video, applications and tickets. 2) Total of accommodation services, fares and package tours. 3) Total of medicines and health foods. 4) Total of cosmetics, private transportation, other goods and services.
Source: Statistics Bureau, MIC.

(4) Electronic Money

Use of electronic money has been increasing, as a means for settling accounts that can be easily used at transportation facilities, convenience stores, supermarkets, etc. Based on two-or-more-person households in the "Survey of Household Economy", the percentage of households with members who owned electronic money and the percentage of households with members who used electronic money have been on an increasing trend starting in 2008. In 2021, the percentage of households with members who owned electronic money was 69.1 percent, and the percentage of households with members who used electronic money was 58.0 percent.

Figure 13.8
Trends in Ownership and Utilization of Electronic Money
(Two-or-more-person households)

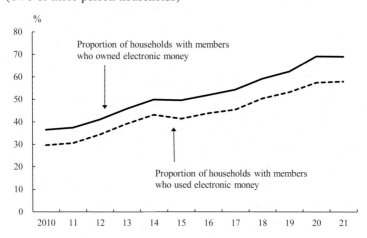

Source: Statistics Bureau, MIC.

2. Prices

Producer prices fell in 2009 due to the bankruptcy of the major American securities firm Lehman Brothers. From 2010 to 2013, prices fluctuated in the range of plus or minus 3 percent, then rose in 2014 due to depreciation of the yen, and fell from 2015 to 2016 due to the decline in international commodity prices and a stronger yen. From 2018 to 2019, there was a drop in global resource prices due to a worldwide economic slowdown brought on by trade friction between the U.S.A. and China, and thus the size of the increase in producer prices contracted. In 2020, producer prices declined with global resource prices due to the COVID-19 pandemic, but from the second quarter of 2021, producer prices began to rise due to rising global resource prices.

Consumer prices began a rising trend in 2008 due to sharp increases in imported raw material prices, but began to fall in 2009 as a result of falling imported raw material prices due to the bankruptcy of the major American securities firm Lehman Brothers, and the trend was generally downwards until 2013. Consumer prices rose due to the increase in the consumption tax to 8 percent in April 2014, but the stimulative effects of the tax increase subsided by the first half of 2015. From the fourth quarter of 2016, the upward trend continued, due to global resource prices (such as crude oil) and exchange rates, but from 2018, trade friction between the U.S.A. and China had a major impact. The consumption tax rate was raised to 10 percent in October 2019, but the increase in consumer prices was less than 1 percent. From the second quarter of 2020, consumer behavior was constrained by the COVID-19 pandemic and domestic demand fell, resulting in a decline in the increase rate of consumer prices, and from the fourth quarter of 2020, consumer prices fell, but then rose from the fourth quarter of 2021.

Figure 13.9
Price Trends (Percent change from previous year)

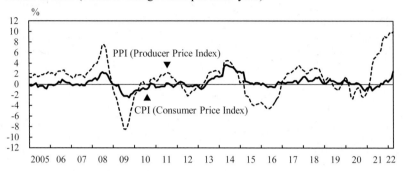

Source: Statistics Bureau, MIC; Bank of Japan.

(1) Consumer Price Index (CPI)

The all items index of consumer prices (with base year 2020 = 100) was 99.8 in 2021, down 0.2 percent from the previous year.

Table 13.5
CPI for Major Categories of Goods and Services

(CY2020=100)

Item	Weight	2005	2010	2015	2019	2021
All items	10000	95.2	94.8	98.2	100.0	99.8
All items, less imputed rent	8420	93.8	93.5	97.8	100.0	99.7
Food	2626	85.9	88.7	94.6	98.7	100.0
Housing	2149	101.1	100.5	99.6	99.4	100.6
Fuel, light and water charges	693	82.2	87.1	101.2	102.5	101.3
Furniture and household utensils	387	115.2	103.2	97.6	97.7	101.7
Clothing and footwear	353	92.4	92.3	96.4	98.9	100.4
Medical care	477	97.1	96.0	95.8	99.7	99.6
Transportation and communication	1493	99.3	97.7	101.2	100.2	95.0
Education	304	112.7	104.9	107.3	108.4	100.0
Culture and recreation	911	105.8	98.1	97.0	100.6	101.6
Miscellaneous	607	89.1	91.8	100.7	102.1	101.1
Goods	5046	92.5	92.4	96.8	99.5	100.8
Services	4954	98.0	97.3	99.6	100.5	98.7

Source: Statistics Bureau, MIC.

According to the general index (all items, less imputed rent) in the regional difference index of consumer prices, which compares the difference in consumer price levels by prefecture, Tokyo had the highest score in 2020, with a figure of 105.2 against the national average set at 100, followed by Kanagawa, with 103.2. On the other hand, Miyazaki registered the lowest score, with 95.9, followed by Gunma with 96.7.

Figure 13.10
Regional Difference Index of Consumer Prices
by Selected Prefectures (2020)   (Japan=100)

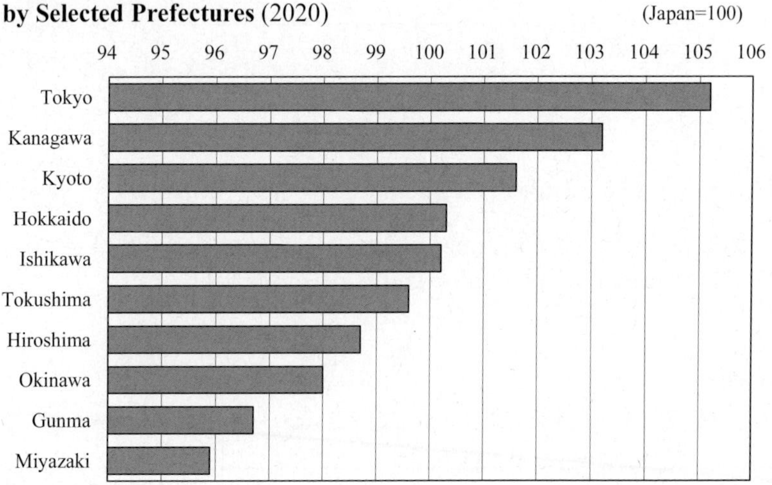

Source: Statistics Bureau, MIC.

(2) Corporate Goods and Services Producer Price Indices

The Corporate Goods Price Index measures price changes of goods traded in the corporate sector. It is comprised of the Producer Price Index (price index of domestically-produced and domestically-traded goods in the corporate sector), the Export Price Index, and the Import Price Index.

In 2021, the Producer Price Index (CY2015 as the base year = 100) was 105.1, up 4.8 percent from the previous year.

In 2021, the Export Price Index increased to 104.4 on a contract currency basis (up 7.2 percent from the previous year), and to 98.6 on a yen basis (up 9.3 percent from the previous year). Furthermore, the Import Price

Index rose to 111.6 on a contract currency basis (up 20.3 percent from the previous year) and to 104.0 on a yen basis (up 22.8 percent from the previous year).

The Services Producer Price Index measures price movements of services traded between companies. In 2021, the Services Producer Price Index (CY2015 as the base year = 100) was 105.1, up 0.9 percent from the previous year.

Table 13.6
Corporate Goods and Services Producer Price Indices

(CY2015=100)

Item	Weight	2017	2018	2019	2020	2021
Corporate Goods Price Index						
Producer Price Index	1000.0	98.7	101.3	101.5	100.3	105.1
Manufacturing industry products	888.3	98.9	101.1	101.2	100.4	105.4
Export Price Index (yen basis)	1000.0	95.5	96.8	93.1	90.2	98.6
Import Price Index (yen basis)	1000.0	92.7	99.7	94.4	84.7	104.0
Services Producer Price Index						
All items	1000.0	101.0	102.2	103.3	104.2	105.1
Information and communications	228.3	100.2	100.9	101.3	102.5	102.7
Transportation and postal activities	158.0	100.2	102.7	104.4	105.6	106.9
Real estate services	94.5	102.4	103.6	104.9	105.6	107.1
Leasing and rental	79.2	99.1	99.2	99.5	100.4	100.4

Source: Bank of Japan.

Chapter 14

Environment and Life

© YANO Keiichi

Police boxes have developed over a long history, and are said to be one reason behind the high level of public security in Japan. These police boxes which originated in Japan have been highly praised by foreign countries as a system for community-based policing.

As a rule, police officers staff each box 24 hours a day, operating in shifts, and to protect the safety of daily life, they engage in a variety of activities, including responding to incidents/accidents, providing directions to passersby, handling lost property, discussing problems, patrolling, and making door-to-door community police visits.

1. Environmental Issues

The list of environmental issues is wide-ranging, from waste management to global warming. Japan is, while pursuing regional development at home, taking the initiative in efforts to prevent global warming and conserve the natural environment to help achieve sustainable growth of the entire world.

In fiscal 2020, Japan's total emission of greenhouse gases, which are a major cause of global warming, amounted to 1.2 billion tons (calculated after their conversion into carbon dioxide), representing a decrease of 5.1 percent from the previous fiscal year. Carbon dioxide accounted for 90.8 percent of these greenhouse gases, with an emission volume of 1.0 billion tons. A breakdown of carbon dioxide emissions by sector revealed that emissions from the industrial sector accounted for 34.0 percent of the total, followed in order by emissions from the transport sector, the commercial industry sector (office buildings, etc.), the residential sector, and the energy industry sector (electric power plants, etc.).

Table 14.1
Breakdown of Carbon Dioxide Emissions [1) 2)]

(Million tons)

Category	FY1990	FY2005	FY2010	FY2015	FY2019	FY2020
Total	1,164	1,294	1,218	1,226	1,108	1,044
Industrial sector	503	467	431	430	387	356
Transport sector	208	244	229	217	206	185
Commercial industry sector	131	220	200	218	191	182
Residential sector	129	171	178	187	159	166
Energy industry sector	96	98	99	93	86	78
Industrial processes and product use	66	57	47	47	45	43
Waste (incineration, etc.)	24	32	29	30	31	31
Others	7	5	4	3	3	3

1) Volume of carbon dioxide after reallocation to the end-use sector. 2) Due to the revision of the Electricity Business Act (liberalization of electricity retail sales), the emission intensity of electricity used in each sector has changed since FY2016.
Source: Ministry of the Environment.

Figure 14.1
Sources of Carbon Dioxide Emissions [1] (FY2020)

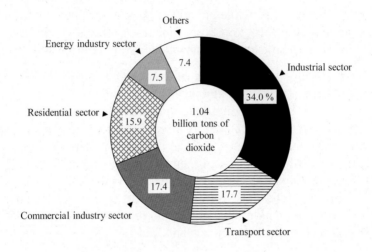

1) Volume of carbon dioxide after reallocation to the end-use sector.
Source: Ministry of the Environment.

The state of waste management in Japan had remained serious due to the shrinking remaining capacity of final disposal sites and increased illegal dumping. This led to the Basic Act on Establishing a Sound Material-Cycle Society (brought into force in January 2001), which defines basic principles for the creation of a sound material-cycle society. This Act has established a legal framework to address issues such as waste disposal and recycling of automobile and electrical appliance. Furthermore, in Japan, the "3Rs" (reduce, reuse and recycle) in waste management including R&D on waste recycling technology and appropriate management of materials of hazards have been promoted, but recently, socio-economic systems have been developed to especially implement the "2Rs" (reduce and reuse) from among the "3Rs".

Of various types of waste generated as a result of business activities, 20 of them, including sludge, waste oil, soot and dust, and imported waste, are designated as "industrial waste". The fiscal 2019 nationwide industrial waste generation totaled 386 million tons. Sludge, animal excreta, and debris, which account for approximately 80 percent of the total industrial waste, are now increasingly recycled into construction materials, fertilizers, and other materials. Thanks to this development, the volume of final disposal (to be put into landfills) fell from 89 million tons in fiscal 1990 to 9 million tons in fiscal 2019.

Meanwhile, a total of 43 million tons of "nonindustrial waste" (household waste and also shop, office, and restaurant waste) was generated in fiscal 2019. This translates to 918 grams per person per day. The total volume of processed nonindustrial waste was 41 million tons in fiscal 2019. The total volume of recycled waste was 8 million tons, with the recycling rate at 19.6 percent.

Table 14.2
Waste Generation and Disposal

(Thousand tons)

Item	FY1990	FY2000	FY2005	FY2010	FY2019
Industrial waste					
Total volume of waste generation	394,736	406,037	421,677	385,988	385,955
Recycling	150,568	184,237	218,888	204,733	203,569
Treatment for waste reduction	154,443	176,933	178,560	167,000	173,228
Final disposal	89,725	44,868	24,229	14,255	9,157
Nonindustrial waste [1]					
Total volume of waste generation	50,257	54,834	52,720	45,359	42,737
Municipally scheduled and collected	42,495	46,695	44,633	38,827	37,020
Directly brought to					
waste treatment facilities	6,776	5,373	5,090	3,803	3,808
Recyclable waste					
collected by community	986	2,765	2,996	2,729	1,909
Waste generated					
daily per person (in grams)	1,115	1,185	1,131	976	918
Total volume of processed waste	49,282	52,090	49,754	42,791	40,949
Direct incineration	36,192	40,304	38,486	33,799	32,947
Intermediate treatment for recycling, etc.	3,300	6,479	7,283	6,161	5,721
Direct recycling		2,224	2,541	2,170	1,884
Direct final disposal	9,790	3,084	1,444	662	398

1) Due to the Great East Japan Earthquake, figures for FY2010 exclude those for Minamisanriku Town, Miyagi Prefecture. Figures for FY2019 exclude disaster waste.
Source: Ministry of the Environment.

Figure 14.2
Recycling of Nonindustrial Waste [1]

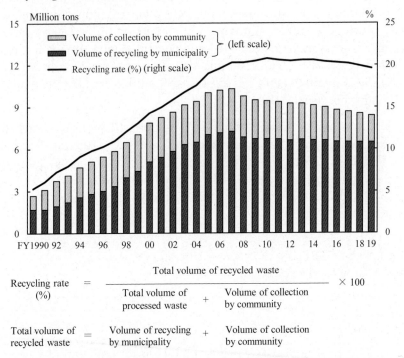

$$\text{Recycling rate (\%)} = \frac{\text{Total volume of recycled waste}}{\text{Total volume of processed waste} + \text{Volume of collection by community}} \times 100$$

$$\text{Total volume of recycled waste} = \text{Volume of recycling by municipality} + \text{Volume of collection by community}$$

1) Due to the Great East Japan Earthquake, figures for FY2010 exclude those for Minamisanriku Town, Miyagi Prefecture. Figures after FY2011 exclude disaster waste.

Source: Ministry of the Environment.

2. Housing

The total number of dwellings (the number of individual units in the case of apartment buildings) in Japan was 62 million in 2018, up by 2 million, 2.9 percent from 2013. The number of households was 54 million, representing the excess in number of dwellings over households by 8 million.

In 2018, the number of occupied dwellings (where people usually live) amounted to 54 million, accounting for 85.9 percent of the total number of dwellings. Of these, the number of dwellings used exclusively for living totaled 53 million, accounting for 98.2 percent of the occupied dwellings. Meanwhile, the number of vacant dwellings increased by 0.3 million, 3.6 percent from 2013, to 8 million. That vacancy rate represented 13.6 percent of the total number of dwellings, the highest-ever ratio.

Figure 14.3

Trends in Dwellings, Vacant Dwellings, and Vacancy Rate

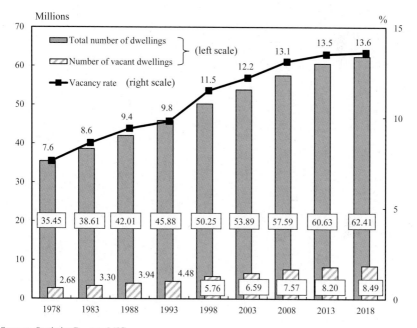

Source: Statistics Bureau, MIC.

A breakdown of occupied dwellings by category of ownership showed that owned houses totaled 33 million, accounting for 61.2 percent of the total, which represented a decrease of 0.5 percentage points from the figure of 61.7 percent in 2013. Rented houses, on the other hand, numbered 19 million, accounting for 35.6 percent of the total.

Table 14.3
Housing Conditions

(Thousands)

Year	Total households	Total number of dwellings [1]	Occupied dwellings [2]	Ownership		Dwellings used exclusively for living	Floor space per dwelling (m^2) [2]
				Owned	Rented		
1988	37,812	42,007	37,413	22,948	14,015	34,701	85.0
1993	41,159	45,879	40,773	24,376	15,691	38,457	88.4
1998	44,360	50,246	43,922	26,468	16,730	41,744	89.6
2003	47,255	53,891	46,863	28,666	17,166	45,258	92.5
2008	49,973	57,586	49,598	30,316	17,770	48,281	92.4
2013	52,453	60,629	52,102	32,166	18,519	50,982	93.0
2018	54,001	62,407	53,616	32,802	19,065	52,642	92.1

1) Including dwellings without occupying households.
2) Including ownership of dwelling "Not reported".
Source: Statistics Bureau, MIC.

Table 14.4
Occupied Dwellings by Type of Building

(Thousands)

Year	Total	Detached houses	Tenement houses	Apartments	Others
1988	37,413	23,311	2,490	11,409	203
1993	40,773	24,141	2,163	14,267	202
1998	43,922	25,269	1,828	16,601	224
2003	46,863	26,491	1,483	18,733	156
2008	49,598	27,450	1,330	20,684	134
2013	52,102	28,599	1,289	22,085	130
2018	53,616	28,759	1,369	23,353	136

Source: Statistics Bureau, MIC.

Occupied dwellings by building type showed that 29 million or 53.6 percent were detached houses, and 23 million or 43.6 percent were apartments. The proportion of apartments has consistently increased in recent years.

In terms of construction materials, 27 million or 92.6 percent of the detached houses were wood-frame houses (including fire-resistant ones). On the other hand, 17 million or 72.3 percent of the apartments were steel-framed concrete structures.

The number of principal households with household members aged 65 years old and over was 22.53 million. Of these households, there were 9.56 million households living in houses that are handrail-equipped at 2 or more locations or have a step-free interior (constant barrier-free houses), accounting for 42.4 percent of households with elderly members. This marked an increase of 1.2 percentage points compared to 2013.

Table 14.5
Ratio of Barrier-Free Houses with Elderly Members

Year	Principal households [1] with household members aged 65 years old and over					
	Number (1,000)			Ratio (%)		
	Total	Constant barrier-free houses [2]	High barrier-free houses [3]	Total	Constant barrier-free houses [2]	High barrier-free houses [3]
2013	20,844	8,584	1,775	100.0	41.2	8.5
2018	22,534	9,556	1,988	100.0	42.4	8.8

1) When a single household lives in 1 house, it is called a "principal household", and if 2 or more households live in 1 house, then the main household from among the multiple households is regarded as the "principal household". 2) Houses that are handrail-equipped at 2 or more locations, or have step-free interiors, as equipment for the elderly etc. 3) Houses that are handrail-equipped at 2 or more locations, and have step-free interiors and wheelchair-accessible hallways, as equipment for the elderly etc.
Source: Statistics Bureau, MIC.

3. Traffic Accidents

In 1970, the annual number of fatalities from traffic accidents hit a record high of 16,765, leading to the enactment of the Traffic Safety Measures Basic Acts in the same year. Based on this, the government has promoted traffic safety measures in a comprehensive and systematic manner. As a result, the number of traffic accident fatalities was 2,839 in 2020, which is the lowest number since 1948 when the current traffic accident statistics were adopted, and this represented approximately one-sixth of the number in 1970.

In 2020, the number of traffic accident fatalities per 100,000 population was 2.3 persons, while that per 10,000 motor vehicles owned was 0.3 persons.

Table 14.6
Traffic Accidents and Casualties

Year	Traffic accidents	Injuries	Traffic accident fatalities [1]	per 10,000 motor vehicles owned	per 100,000 population
1970	718,080	981,096	16,765	9.0	16.2
1980	476,677	598,719	8,760	2.2	7.5
1990	643,097	790,295	11,227	1.9	9.1
2000	931,950	1,155,707	9,073	1.2	7.1
2010	725,924	896,297	4,948	0.6	3.9
2019	381,237	461,775	3,215	0.4	2.5
2020	309,178	369,476	2,839	0.3	2.3

1) Death within 24 hours of the accident.
Source: Cabinet Office.

4. Crime

The police organization consists of the National Public Safety Commission and the National Police Agency, both of which are state organizations, as well as the Prefectural Public Safety Commission and prefectural police, both of which are organizations under the authority of individual prefectures. As of April 1, 2021, the prefectural police operated police headquarters, police academies, 1,149 police stations, 6,253 police boxes and 6,185 police substations in 47 prefectures.

Community police officers at their respective police boxes/substations are engaged in standing guard over their communities, patrolling, and dealing with criminal cases and accidents to prevent crime and catch criminals.

In 2021, the reported number of penal code offenses was 568,104, a decrease of 46,127, or 7.5 percent compared to the previous year. The proportion of thefts was the highest, accounting for 67.2 percent, or 381,769 cases (down 8.5 percent from the previous year).

The number of persons arrested for penal code offenses was 175,041 in 2021, a decrease of 7,541, or 4.1 percent compared to the previous year, marking a decline for the 17th consecutive year.

The ratio of arrests to reported number of offenses marked 19.8 percent in 2001, the lowest since World War II. From 2002 to 2007, this ratio increased, and levelled off afterwards. From 2014 it exhibited a rising trend, and in 2021, it was 46.6 percent, an increase of 1.1 percentage points from the previous year.

Table 14.7
Trends in Crime (Penal code offenses)

Year	Reported offenses	Resultant arrests	Persons arrested	Arrest rate [1] (%)	Crime rate per 100,000 population
1980	1,357,461	811,189	392,113	59.8	1,159.6
1985	1,607,697	1,032,879	432,250	64.2	1,328.1
1990	1,636,628	692,593	293,264	42.3	1,324.0
1995	1,782,944	753,174	293,252	42.2	1,419.5
2000	2,443,470	576,771	309,649	23.6	1,925.5
2005	2,269,293	649,503	386,955	28.6	1,775.7
2010	1,604,019	497,356	322,620	31.0	1,252.6
2015	1,098,969	357,484	239,355	32.5	864.7
2020	614,231	279,185	182,582	45.5	486.6
2021	568,104	264,485	175,041	46.6	452.7

1) The ratio of arrests to reported number of offenses.
Source: National Police Agency; Ministry of Justice.

Various kinds of computers and computer networks are currently playing an essential role as a social foundation. In line with this, crimes utilizing computer networks are becoming increasingly diversified. The number of arrests for cybercrime (violation of the Unauthorized Computer Access Act, offenses involving computers or electromagnetic records, offenses related to creation of unauthorized commands for electromagnetic records, etc.) in 2021 was 12,209, up 23.6 percent from the previous year. This represented about a thirteenfold increase from the 913 cases registered in 2000.

Chapter 15

Social Security, Health Care, and Public Hygiene

© DATE Kanetoshi

A happy moment of daily life. In Japan, there are many sprightly elderly people who can live independently. As of 2019, health life expectancy, the average period without being restricted in daily life, ranks among the highest in the world at 75.4 years for women, and 72.7 years for men.

1. Social Security

In Japan, the birth rate has been falling, while the number of elderly people has been growing. Meanwhile, its social security system is required to address various changes in the socioeconomic environment.

In April 2000, a long-term care insurance system was launched. When the system was first established, there were 2.18 million people certified as needing care or needing support. This number grew by approximately 3.1-fold, to 6.84 million people as of April 2021, and the long-term care insurance system has become anchored in society. Today, there are approaches aimed at enhancing services for promoting "the Community-based Integrated Care System" (system where medical care, nursing care, preventive care, and livelihood support are provided integrally in regions where one is used to living), as well as realizing a local, inclusive society.

The number of monthly users of long-term care insurance services totaled, on average, 5.67 million per month in fiscal 2019, and increased by approximately 3.1-fold over 19 years in comparison to the approximately 1.84 million users in fiscal 2000, when the system was initiated. In addition, the amount of nursing care costs in fiscal 2019 (including allowances for high-cost long-term care service, for high-cost medical care and long-term care service, and for long-term care service to a person admitted to a specified facility), totaled 10.8 trillion yen.

Table 15.1

Trends in Social Security Benefit Expenditures by Functional Category [1) 2) 3) 4) 5)]

(Billion yen)

Item	FY2000	FY2005	FY2010	FY2015	FY2018	FY2019
Total	78,406	88,853	105,365	116,813	121,399	123,924
Old age	36,688	# 44,102	51,335	# 55,339	57,277	57,835
Survivors	5,958	# 6,459	6,795	# 6,670	6,498	6,450
Invalidity benefits	2,151	# 2,397	3,398	# 4,283	4,751	4,900
Employment injury	1,058	984	943	# 919	918	930
Sickness and health	25,576	# 27,490	32,213	# 36,890	38,083	39,082
Family benefits	2,365	# 3,232	5,009	# 7,142	8,489	9,191
Unemployment	2,647	1,453	2,250	1,442	1,430	1,463
Housing	201	# 429	513	617	603	603
Other social policy areas	1,761	# 2,307	2,910	# 3,510	3,350	3,470

1) This table is calculated in accordance with the standards of the ILO's "The Cost of Social Security 19th International Inquiry."

2) Because of retrospective tabulation up to FY2005 of expenditure items data that were added in FY2011, a gap has occurred with FY2004 data.

3) Since FY2011, Employees' Accident Compensation has been added for special national public servants in the House of Representatives, House of Councillors, National Diet Library, courts, Ministry of Foreign Affairs, and Ministry of Defense.

4) In addition to expenses for early childhood care services, expenses for early childhood education are included in total social security benefit expenditures from FY2015.

5) There is a gap between FY2014 and FY2015 because of the change in the scope of the services operated independently by local public entities that were targeted for tabulation in FY2015.

Source: National Institute of Population and Social Security Research.

In fiscal 2019, social security benefit expenditures totaled 123.9 trillion yen (up 2.1 percent from the previous fiscal year), a figure which amounted to 982,200 yen per person. The ratio of Japan's social security benefit expenditures to national income registered 30.9 percent. Benefits for the aged accounted for 66.2 percent of total social security benefit expenditures.

Figure 15.1
Trends in Social Security Benefit Expenditures by Sector ^{1) 2) 3) 4)}

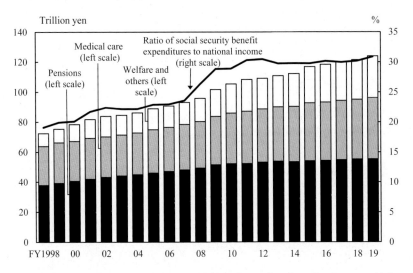

1) Because of retrospective tabulation up to FY2005 of expenditure items data that were added in FY2011, a gap has occurred with FY2004 data.
2) Since FY2011, Employees' Accident Compensation has been added for special national public servants in the House of Representatives, House of Councillors, National Diet Library, courts, Ministry of Foreign Affairs, and Ministry of Defense.
3) In addition to expenses for early childhood care services, expenses for early childhood education are included in total social security benefit expenditures from FY2015.
4) There is a gap between FY2014 and FY2015 because of the change in the scope of the services operated independently by local public entities that were targeted for tabulation in FY2015.
Source: National Institute of Population and Social Security Research.

In fiscal 2019, pensions accounted for 44.7 percent of total social security benefit expenditures, while medical care accounted for 32.9 percent, and social welfare and others for 22.4 percent. Social security benefit expenditures are forecasted to continue growing.

In accordance with the rise in social security benefit expenditures, the amount of social insurance contributions and taxes has also increased, reaching 132.4 trillion yen in fiscal 2019. This was financed by 74.0 trillion yen from social insurance contributions, 51.9 trillion yen from taxes and 6.5 trillion yen from other sources. The government has established "Social Security for All Generations", in which all generations support each other fairly, and is examining sustainable reforms.

The national contribution ratio (the combined ratios of taxes and social security costs to national income) was 47.9 percent in fiscal 2020 (taxation burden: 28.2 percent; social security premiums: 19.7 percent), up 3.5 percentage points from 44.4 percent in fiscal 2019 (taxation burden: 25.8 percent; social security premiums: 18.6 percent). The national contribution ratio in 2019 was 32.4 percent in the U.S.A., 46.5 percent in the U.K., and 67.1 percent in France. While the ratio in Japan was higher than that of the U.S.A., it was lower than European countries.

Figure 15.2
National Contribution Ratio by Country

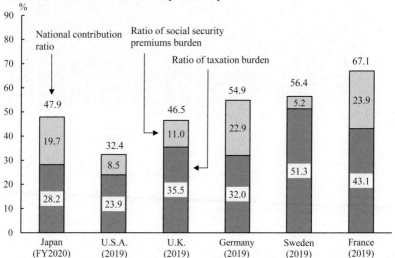

Source: Ministry of Finance.

2. Health Care and Public Hygiene

Japan has a universal health insurance regime to ensure that anyone can receive necessary medical treatment. Under this regime, every citizen enters a publicly regulated medical insurance system, such as employees' health insurance, national health insurance or the latter-stage elderly's medical insurance.

This medical care system has contributed to Japan's achieving the highest life expectancy in the world, as well as a high standard of healthcare along with improvements in the living environment and better nutrition.

Currently, reform of the whole system is being undertaken in order to preserve the stability of this medical insurance system in the future.

Life expectancy at birth was 87.7 years for women and 81.6 years for men in 2020. Japan's life expectancy remains at a high level in the world. Even with regard to healthy life expectancy, which is the "average period without being restricted in daily life", Japan was among the world's highest as of 2019, with 75.4 years for women and 72.7 years for men. Japan's infant mortality rate was 1.8 per 1,000 births in 2020.

Figure 15.3
Death Rates by Major Cause

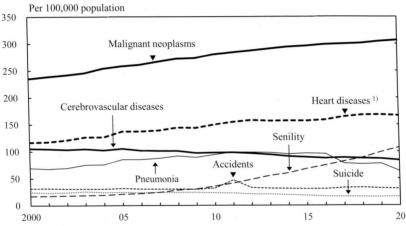

1) Excluding hypertensive diseases.
Source: Ministry of Health, Labour and Welfare.

The death rate was 1,112.5 per 100,000 population in 2020. The leading cause of death was malignant neoplasms (306.6 per 100,000 population), followed by lifestyle diseases such as heart diseases (166.6; excluding hypertensive diseases), in which people's daily diet and behavior are significant factors, and senility (107.3). Malignant neoplasms became the leading cause of death in 1981. The death rate by malignant neoplasms has continued to increase since, reaching 27.6 percent of all deaths in 2020.

The number of deaths caused by suicide in Japan hovered at around 30,000 annually in 1998 and onwards. In recent years, the number has remained steady at around 20,000. The number of suicides in 2020 was 20,243. In 2020, suicide was the leading cause of deaths for people aged between 10 and 39.

In the past, human beings have faced the threat of various epidemic diseases, including new strains of influenza. In 2014, cases of infection from Dengue fever in Japan were confirmed for the first time in approximately 70 years. In 2018, the number of patients with rubella increased. In 2020, the outbreak of COVID-19 developed into a pandemic, resulting in increasing numbers of infections and verified deaths. Currently, in Japan, infection control measures are being advanced, such as through the implementation of vaccinations, with the objective of preventing the occurrence and spread of infectious diseases.

In terms of healthcare provision, Japan had 336,882 physicians engaged in medical care, or 267.0 physicians per 100,000 population, in 2020. While the number of physicians providing healthcare is increasing nationwide, their uneven distribution has become a problem due to the lack of physicians specializing in certain areas of medicine and the lack of physicians operating in regional parts of the country.

Table 15.2
Medical Personnel at Work

Personnel	2012	2014	2016	2018	2020
Number					
Physicians	300,664	308,651	317,162	324,737	336,822
Dentists	101,110	102,534	103,127	103,418	105,798
Pharmacists	262,520	271,364	284,069	294,430	302,504
Nurses and Assistant nurses	1,373,521	1,426,932	1,472,508	1,523,085	1,565,500
Rates per 100,000 population					
Physicians	235.6	242.6	249.7	256.2	267.0
Dentists	79.2	80.6	81.2	81.6	83.9
Pharmacists	205.7	213.3	223.6	232.3	239.8
Nurses and Assistant nurses	1,076.5	1,121.5	1,159.1	1,201.7	1,241.0

Source: Statistics Bureau, MIC; Ministry of Health, Labour and Welfare.

As of October 1, 2020, the number of hospitals in Japan (excluding medical clinics and dental clinics) totaled 8,238. The number of hospital beds amounted to 1,507,526 (1,195.1 per 100,000 population).

Table 15.3
Medical Care Institutions and Beds

Type of Institution	2011	2014	2017	2019	2020
Institutions					
Total	176,308	177,546	178,492	179,416	178,724
Hospitals	8,605	8,493	8,412	8,300	8,238
Medical clinics	99,547	100,461	101,471	102,616	102,612
Dental clinics	68,156	68,592	68,609	68,500	67,874
Rates per 100,000 population					
Total	138.0	139.7	140.9	142.2	141.7
Hospitals	6.7	6.7	6.6	6.6	6.5
Medical clinics	77.9	79.1	80.1	81.3	81.3
Dental clinics	53.3	54.0	54.1	54.3	.53.8
Beds					
Total	1,712,539	1,680,712	1,653,303	1,620,097	1,593,633
Hospitals	1,583,073	1,568,261	1,554,879	1,529,215	1,507,526
Medical clinics	129,366	112,364	98,355	90,825	86,046
Dental clinics	100	87	69	57	61
Rates per 100,000 population					
Total	1,340.0	1,322.5	1,304.8	1,284.1	1,263.3
Hospitals	1,238.7	1,234.0	1,227.2	1,212.1	1,195.1
Medical clinics	101.2	88.4	77.6	72.0	68.2
Dental clinics	0.1	0.1	0.1	0.0	0.0

Source: Ministry of Health, Labour and Welfare.

In fiscal 2019, national medical care expenditures totaled 44.4 trillion yen or 11.06 percent of Japan's national income. The cost of medical care per person averaged 351,800 yen in fiscal 2019.

Medical costs for treating the latter-stage elderly in fiscal 2018 were 16.4 trillion yen, or 37.8 percent of national medical care expenditure, and accounted for 4.08 percent of the national income. The per-capita cost of medical care for the latter-stage elderly averaged 943,082 yen for the year. The percentage of national medical care expenditures accounted for by medical care costs for the late-stage elderly decreased when the age of persons eligible to receive later-stage elderly medical care was raised in a phased manner over 5 years from 70 years to 75 years old in October 2002, but in recent years, there has been a slight uptrend.

Figure 15.4
Trends in Medical Care Expenditures

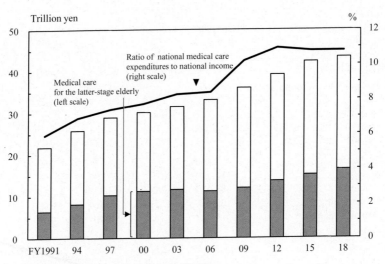

Source: Ministry of Health, Labour and Welfare.

Chapter 16

Education and Culture

© KITAMURA Shuichi

According to the "2016 Survey on Time Use and Leisure Activities", the total number of people aged 10 years old and over who participated in some kind of sports was 77,977,000, for a participation rate of 68.8 percent. The total number of participants in basketball was 4,864,000, for a participation rate of 4.3 percent.

1. School-Based Education

Japan's primary and secondary education is based on a 6-3-3 system: 6 years in elementary school, 3 years in lower secondary school, and 3 years in upper secondary school. The period of compulsory schooling is the 9 years at elementary and lower secondary schools. Higher education institutions are universities, junior colleges, and colleges of technology. Other education establishments include kindergartens and integrated centers for early childhood education and care, which provide pre-school education, and schools for special needs education. There are also specialized training colleges and miscellaneous schools for a wide range of vocational and other practical skills learning. In order to promote diversity of the school education system, unified lower-upper secondary schooling began at some schools in 1999. Furthermore, in 2016, compulsory education schools, where compulsory education for elementary schools to lower secondary schools is carried out consistently, were established. On an additional note, the school year in Japan starts in April and ends in March of the following year.

Table 16.1

Educational Institutions in Japan (as of May 1, 2021)

Type of institution	Schools				Full-time teachers (1,000)	Students (1,000)	
	Total	National	Public	Private		Males	Females
Kindergartens	9,418	49	3,103	6,266	90	510	499
Integrated centers for early childhood education and care	6,269	-	862	5,407	129	408	389
Elementary schools	19,336	67	19,028	241	423	3,184	3,040
Lower secondary schools	10,076	68	9,230	778	248	1,652	1,578
Compulsory education schools	151	5	145	1	5	30	28
Upper secondary schools	4,856	15	3,521	1,320	227	1,521	1,488
Secondary schools	56	4	34	18	3	16	17
Schools for special needs education [1]	1,160	45	1,100	15	86	96	50
Colleges of technology	57	51	3	3	4	45	12
Junior colleges	315	-	14	301	7	13	90
Universities	803	86	98	619	190	1,621	1,297
Graduate schools	652	86	86	480	107	173	84
Specialized training colleges	3,083	8	186	2,889	41	292	370
Miscellaneous schools	1,069	-	5	1,064	9	55	48

1) Schools for mentally and/or physically challenged children, inclusive of kindergarten to upper secondary school levels.

Source: Ministry of Education, Culture, Sports, Science and Technology.

Figure 16.1
Japanese School System

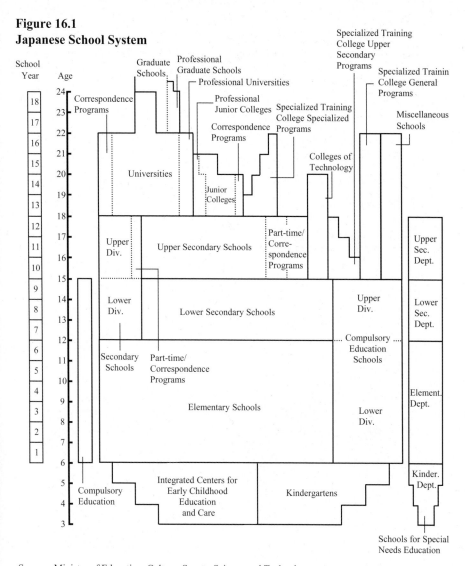

Source: Ministry of Education, Culture, Sports, Science and Technology.

Of the March 2021 upper secondary school and upper division of secondary school graduates, 57.5 percent went straight on to enter a university, junior college, etc. The ratio of graduates of upper secondary school, etc. who entered a university or junior college in 2021 was 58.9 percent (59.0 percent of male and 58.8 percent of female graduates), including graduates from previous years.

Table 16.2
Number of University Students (as of May 1)

	2010	2015	2019	2020	2021
Total	2,887,414	2,860,210	2,918,668	2,915,605	2,917,998
Undergraduate	2,559,191	2,556,062	2,609,148	2,623,572	2,625,688
Graduate schools	271,454	249,474	254,621	254,529	257,128
Others [1]	56,769	54,674	54,899	37,504	35,182
Females	1,185,580	1,231,868	1,293,095	1,294,320	1,297,056
Undergraduate	1,077,782	1,127,372	1,183,962	1,193,465	1,196,555
Graduate schools	82,133	77,831	82,427	82,982	84,017
Others [1]	25,665	26,665	26,706	17,873	16,484
National	625,048	610,802	606,449	598,881	597,450
Public	142,523	148,766	158,176	158,579	160,438
Private	2,119,843	2,100,642	2,154,043	2,158,145	2,160,110

1) "Others" include advanced students, short-term students, non-degree students, auditing students and research students.
Source: Ministry of Education, Culture, Sports, Science and Technology.

Figure 16.2
University Students by Field of Study (as of May 1, 2021)

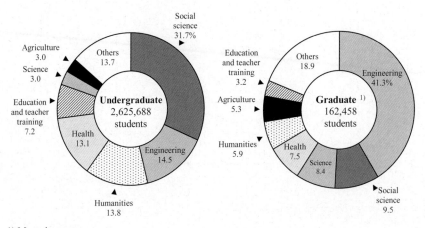

1) Master's course.
Source: Ministry of Education, Culture, Sports, Science and Technology.

As of May 1, 2020, a total of 135,710 foreign students were enrolled in Japanese junior colleges, universities, and graduate schools. Of the total foreign students, 92.1 percent were from Asia, including 75,620 from China, 13,409 from Vietnam and 12,093 from the Republic of Korea.

Fiscal 2018 public expenditure on education in Japan was 23 trillion yen, which is equivalent to 14.0 percent of the net expenditure of national and local governments.

Figure 16.3
Public Expenditures on Education

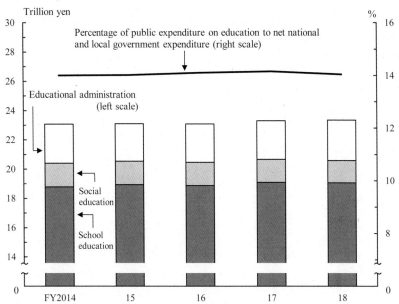

Source: Ministry of Education, Culture, Sports, Science and Technology.

Fiscal 2018 school expenditure by households with children attending public school averaged 63,102 yen per elementary school pupil, 138,961 yen per lower-secondary school student and 280,487 yen per upper-secondary school student.

2. Lifelong Learning

As society approaches a major turning point in heading towards a "100-year-life", there is increasing importance in realizing a "Lifelong Learning Society" in which people are able to select learning opportunities whenever they want during their life, and their learning outcomes are evaluated appropriately.

Today, in order to develop a society where people can engage in learning any time they like throughout their lives, efforts are being made to provide learning opportunities such as school education, social education, cultural activities, sports activities, recreational activities, volunteer activities, and corporate in-house education. In providing places and opportunities for such lifelong learning, educational institutions and social education facilities (citizens' public halls, libraries, museums, and sports facilities, etc.) play a vital role.

Table 16.3
Social Education Facilities and Users

Facilities	Number [1]		Users (1,000) [2]	
	2015	2018	2014	2017
Citizens' public halls [3]	14,841	14,281	193,464	166,517
Libraries [4]	3,331	3,360	181,364	177,899
Museums	1,256	1,286	129,579	142,456
General museums	152	154	8,499	9,349
Science museums	106	104	16,439	16,830
Historical museums	451	470	22,950	28,611
Art museums	441	453	30,724	39,811
Outdoor museums	16	16	2,601	2,157
Zoological gardens	35	34	20,631	19,396
Botanical gardens	10	11	860	1,117
Zoological and botanical gardens	7	6	4,498	4,538
Aquariums	38	38	22,377	20,646
Facilities similar to museums	4,434	4,452	150,417	160,613
Centers for children and youths	941	891	20,058	19,729
Women's education centers	367	358	9,716	11,310
Public sports facilities	47,536	46,981	501,557	526,725
Private sports facilities	14,987	16,397	123,630	107,939
Theaters, concert halls, etc.	1,851	1,827	…	…
Lifelong learning centers	449	478	26,218	27,290

1) As of October 1. 2) Total of fiscal year. 3) Including similar facilities.
4) Including the same type of facilities.
Source: Ministry of Education, Culture, Sports, Science and Technology.

3. Leisure Activities

The results of the "2016 Survey on Time Use and Leisure Activities" conducted on people living in this country, aged 10 years old and over, show that the amount of free time each person has spent was 6 hours and 22 minutes, which was the time remaining after activities that were physiologically necessary (sleeping, eating, etc.) and societally essential (work, housework, etc.).

Table 16.4
Major Leisure Activities by Sex (Aged 10 years old and over) (2016)

Leisure Activities	Total	Males	Females
Free time per day (hours. minutes)	6.22	6.36	6.09
Participation rate (%) [1]			
Hobbies and amusements	87.0	87.2	86.8
Travel and excursion	73.5	71.1	75.8
Sports [2][3]	68.8	73.5	64.4
Learning, self-education, and training [2][4]	36.9	36.5	37.4
Volunteer activities	26.0	25.0	26.9

1) Participants in the activity / Population × 100. 2) Including club activities at school.
3) Excluding sports performed by professional players as their job and by students in PE class. 4) Excluding worker training at the workplace, and study and research activities performed by children, pupils or students as schoolwork, such as study in class, preparation for class and review of lessons.
Source: Statistics Bureau, MIC.

The participation rate for "hobbies and amusements" was 87.0 percent (percentage of people (aged 10 years old and over) who engaged in the activity within the past 12 months), and by sex, the participation rate for males was 87.2 percent and that for females was 86.8 percent. In addition, for participation rates by type of activity, "watching movies other than movie theater" was the highest at 52.1 percent, followed by "listening to music by CD, smartphone, etc." at 49.0 percent, "watching movies in a movie theater" at 39.6 percent, and so on.

The participation rate for "sports" was 68.8 percent, and by sex, the participation rate for males was 73.5 percent and that for females was 64.4 percent. In addition, for participation rates by type of sport, "walking or light physical exercise" was the highest at 41.3 percent, followed by "training with gym equipment" at 14.7 percent, and so on.

Figure 16.4
Participation Rates for Major "Sports" that Showed Participation Rate Increase by Age Group

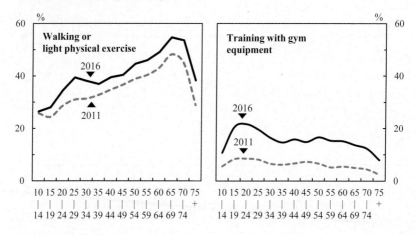

Source: Statistics Bureau, MIC.

4. Publishing and Mass Media

A total of 68,608 new book titles were released in 2020. The number of magazine titles published was 2,626 (including 2,542 monthlies and 84 weeklies). In recent years, the electronic books market has been growing.

Table 16.5
Number of New Book Titles Published

Subject	2016	2017	2018	2019	2020
Total	75,039	73,057	71,661	71,903	68,608
General works	763	858	767	804	805
Philosophy	4,176	3,932	3,955	3,743	3,507
History and geology	3,685	3,404	3,530	3,890	3,927
Social sciences	16,078	15,422	15,220	15,482	14,068
Natural sciences	5,639	5,757	5,325	5,066	5,117
Technology and engineering	4,391	4,176	3,906	3,951	3,608
Industry and commerce	2,625	2,652	2,492	2,444	2,310
Art and life	13,299	12,676	11,856	12,383	12,068
Languages	1,604	1,628	1,535	1,473	1,329
Literature	13,270	13,327	13,048	12,979	12,104
Children's books	4,319	4,350	4,721	4,583	4,295
School textbooks	5,190	4,875	5,306	5,105	5,470

Source: The Research Institute for Publications, The All Japan Magazine and Book
Publisher's and Editor's Association.

Figure 16.5
Trends in the Size of the Electronic Publication Market

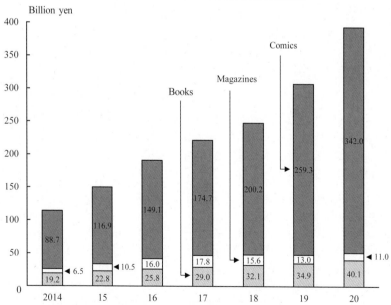

Source: The Research Institute for Publications, The All Japan Magazine and Book Publisher's
and Editor's Association.

A total of 113 daily newspapers were in circulation, and the penetration rate was 0.57 newspapers per household as of October 2021.

Figure 16.6
Trends in the Circulation of Newspaper [1] [2]

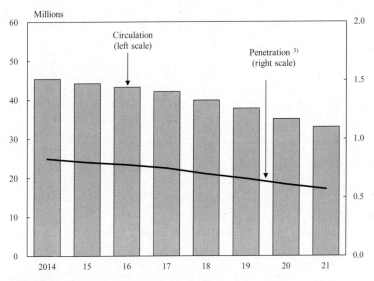

1) As of October. 2) Set paper counted as one copy.
3) Circulation per household. Number of households used for calculation are derived from the Basic Resident Registration as of January 1 of the year.
Source: The Japan Newspaper Publishers and Editors Association.

Japan has a public broadcasting network (NHK: Nippon Hoso Kyokai, or Japan Broadcasting Corporation), as well as commercial networks. NHK is the pioneer broadcasting station in Japan, and has been funded through fees paid by subscribers.

Major broadcasting services can be divided roughly into 3 categories: terrestrial, satellite, and cable television. Terrestrial digital broadcasting was launched in some areas of the Kanto, Kinki and Chukyo regions in December 2003 and then also in other areas, including all prefectural capitals, in December 2006. By March 31, 2012, analog broadcasting ended and was completely replaced with terrestrial digital broadcasting in all parts of Japan. Currently, 4K and 8K broadcast services with 4 and 16 times the pixel number of existing full high definition are being promoted, and new 4K and 8K satellite broadcast services began in December 2018.

In 2021, advertising expenditures in the 4 major mass media types in Japan (newspapers, magazines, radio and television) totaled 2.5 trillion yen, up compared with the previous year. This accounted for 36.1 percent of total advertising expenditures, which were 6.8 trillion yen. Spending on Internet advertising reached 2.7 trillion yen (up 21.4 percent from the previous year). This amounted to 39.8 percent of the total advertising expenditures.

Table 16.6
Advertising Expenditures by Medium

Year	Total	News-papers	Maga-zines	Radio	Tele-vision [1]	Satellite media-related	Internet	Promo-tional media
Advertising expenditures (billion yen)								
2010	5,842.7	639.6	273.3	129.9	1,732.1	78.4	774.7	2,214.7
2015	6,171.0	567.9	244.3	125.4	1,932.3	-	1,159.4	2,141.7
2019	6,938.1	454.7	167.5	126.0	1,861.2	-	# 2,104.8	# 2,223.9
2020	6,159.4	368.8	122.3	106.6	1,655.9	-	2,229.0	1,676.8
2021	6,799.8	381.5	122.4	110.6	1,839.3	-	2,705.2	1,640.8
Percentage distribution (%)								
2010	100.0	11.0	4.7	2.2	29.6	1.3	13.3	37.9
2015	100.0	9.2	4.0	2.0	31.3	-	18.8	34.7
2019	100.0	6.6	2.4	1.8	26.8	-	30.3	32.1
2020	100.0	6.0	2.0	1.7	26.9	-	36.2	27.2
2021	100.0	5.6	1.8	1.6	27.1	-	39.8	24.1

1) Television including Satellite media-related advertising after 2015.
Source: Dentsu Inc.

5. Cultural Assets

Throughout its long history, Japan has been endowed with an abundance of valuable cultural assets, including works of art, historic landmarks, and many natural monuments. To pass on this cultural heritage to future generations, the Japanese government has accorded many of the most important assets as national treasures, designated important cultural properties, historic sites, places of scenic beauty, or natural monuments, based on the Act on Protection of Cultural Properties. In addition to preserving cultural assets, measures to utilize such assets are being established, such as expansion of viewing opportunities through exhibitions.

Table 16.7
Cultural Properties Designated by the National Government
(as of June 1, 2022)

Type of cultural properties	Number	
Important cultural properties	13,360	a) 1,131
Fine arts and crafts	10,820	a) 902
Structures	2,540	a) 229
Historic sites, places of scenic beauty and natural monuments	3,337	b) 174
Historic sites	1,872	b) 63
Places of scenic beauty	427	b) 36
Natural monuments	1,038	b) 75
Important tangible folk cultural properties	225	
Important intangible folk cultural properties	327	
Important intangible cultural properties		
Individual recognition	73	
Performing arts	36	
Craft techniques	37	
Group recognition	30	
Performing arts	14	
Craft techniques	16	
Traditional building preservation areas	126	

a) National treasures only. b) Specially designated places only.
Source: Agency for Cultural Affairs.

As of June 1, 2022, 13,360 items were designated as important cultural properties, of which 1,131 were classified as national treasures. In addition, the government has provided support for such activities as theatrical performances, music, handicrafts, and other important intangible cultural properties. It also has worked to preserve important folk-cultural properties, such as annual cultural events and folk performing arts, as well as to train people to carry on such traditions.

Japan accepted the UNESCO World Heritage Convention (the Convention Concerning the Protection of the World Cultural and Natural Heritage) in 1992.

In July 2021, two new sites were registered in the World Heritage List: Amami-Oshima Island, Tokunoshima Island, Northern part of Okinawa Island, and Iriomote Island; and Jomon Prehistoric Sites in Northern Japan.

Amami-Oshima Island, Tokunoshima Island, Northern Part of Okinawa Island, and Iriomote Island are natural heritage. They have a mild, humid subtropical climate, and are regions inhabited by distinctive land animals, including many endemic species and endangered species.

The Jomon Prehistoric Sites in Northern Japan are cultural heritage consisting of 17 historic sites. These sites present the daily life and spiritual culture of people who lived in the region for more than 10,000 years through hunting, gathering, and fishing.

Table 16.8

Heritage Sites Inscribed on the World Heritage List [1]

Year	Type of heritage	World heritage	Prefecture
1993	Cultural	Buddhist Monuments in the Horyu-ji Area	Nara
	Cultural	Himeji-jo (castle)	Hyogo
	Natural	Shirakami-Sanchi (mountains)	Aomori, Akita
	Natural	Yakushima (island)	Kagoshima
1994	Cultural	Historic Monuments of Ancient Kyoto	Kyoto, Shiga
1995	Cultural	Historic Villages of Shirakawa-go and Gokayama	Gifu, Toyama
1996	Cultural	Hiroshima Peace Memorial (Genbaku Dome)	Hiroshima
	Cultural	Itsukushima Shinto Shrine	Hiroshima
1998	Cultural	Historic Monuments of Ancient Nara	Nara
1999	Cultural	Shrines and Temples of Nikko	Tochigi
2000	Cultural	Gusuku Sites and Related Properties of the Kingdom of Ryukyu	Okinawa
2004	Cultural	Sacred Sites and Pilgrimage Routes in the Kii Mountain Range	Mie, Nara, Wakayama
2005	Natural	Shiretoko (peninsula)	Hokkaido
2007	Cultural	Iwami Ginzan Silver Mine and its Cultural Landscape	Shimane
2011	Cultural	Hiraizumi-Temples, Gardens and Archaeological Sites Representing the Buddhist Pure Land	Iwate
	Natural	Ogasawara Islands	Tokyo
2013	Cultural	Fujisan, Sacred Place and Source of Artistic Inspiration	Yamanashi, Shizuoka
2014	Cultural	Tomioka Silk Mill and Related Sites	Gunma
2015	Cultural	Sites of Japan's Meiji Industrial Revolution: Iron and Steel, Shipbuilding and Coal Mining	Fukuoka, Saga, Nagasaki, Kumamoto, Kagoshima, Yamaguchi, Iwate, Shizuoka
2016	Cultural	The National Museum of Western Art - The Architectural Work of Le Corbusier, an Outstanding Contribution to the Modern Movement	Tokyo
2017	Cultural	Sacred Island of Okinoshima and Associated Sites in the Munakata Region	Fukuoka
2018	Cultural	Hidden Christian Sites in the Nagasaki Region	Nagasaki, Kumamoto
2019	Cultural	Mozu-Furuichi Kofun Group: Mounded Tombs of Ancient Japan	Osaka
2021	Natural	Amami-Oshima Island, Tokunoshima Island, Northern part of Okinawa Island, and Iriomote Island	Kagoshima, Okinawa
	Cultural	Jomon Prehistoric Sites in Northern Japan	Hokkaido, Aomori, Iwate, Akita

1) As of July, 2021.
Source: Agency for Cultural Affairs.

In 2006, the UNESCO Convention for the Safeguarding of the Intangible Cultural Heritage entered into force. As of January 2022, Japan has 22 entries on its list, including: Nogaku Theater, Ningyo Johruri Bunraku Puppet Theater, Kabuki Theater (the kind of Kabuki performed using a traditional method of acting and directing), and Washoku, the traditional dietary culture of Japan.

Chapter 17

Government System

© TODA Remi

On September 1, 2021, the Digital Agency was launched as a "control tower" for realizing a digital society in Japan. The agency drives efforts to promote digitalization of society as whole, in collaboration with national and local governments, the private sector, and other stakeholders. The objective is a digital society realizing diverse forms of happiness for each individual.

1. Separation of Powers

The Constitution of Japan, which went into effect on May 3, 1947, is based on three core principles: sovereignty of the people, respect for fundamental human rights and pacifism. To control governmental power effectively through checks and balances, governmental power is separated into three independent branches: legislative, executive and judicial, and each contains a separate set of agencies and personnel.

Figure 17.1
Separation of Powers under the Constitution of Japan

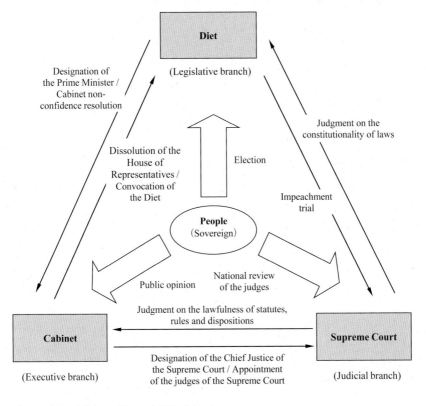

Source: Prime Minister of Japan and His Cabinet.

Figure 17.2
Government Organization [1] (FY2022)

〔Legislative branch〕

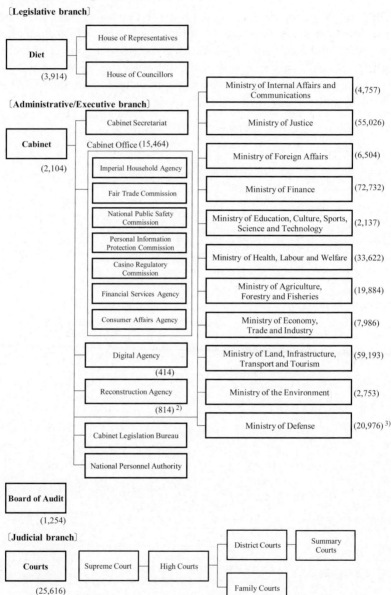

〔Administrative/Executive branch〕

〔Judicial branch〕

1) Figures in parentheses refer to budgetary fixed number of national government employees.
2) Of the 814 employees, 211 are from the Reconstruction Agency and 603 are from other ministries.
3) Excluding the number of the personnel of the Self-Defense Forces.
Source: Cabinet Bureau of Personnel Affairs, Cabinet Secretariat; Ministry of Finance.

2. Legislative Branch

The Diet is the highest organ of state power, and is the sole law-making organ of the State. The Diet consists of the House of Representatives and the House of Councillors. Both Houses consist of elected members, representative of all the people.

The most important responsibility of the Diet is to enact legislation. The Diet also has the authority to fulfill a number of additional functions, including the deliberation and passage of the budget and other matters of fiscal importance, the approval of treaties, the designation of the Prime Minister and the initiation of motions to amend the Constitution. Each House may conduct investigations relating to the government, and demand the presence and testimony of witnesses, and the production of records. For the Diet to pass a resolution, the agreement of both Houses of the Diet is necessary. However, when the two Houses differ in their resolutions regarding legislative bills, draft budgets, the approval of treaties or the designation of the Prime Minister, under the terms of the Constitution, the decision of the House of Representatives overrides that of the House of Councillors.

The term of office for Diet members is set by the Constitution. Members of the House of Representatives serve a 4-year term, while members of the House of Councillors, 6 years. Elections for the latter are held every 3 years, so that one half of the seats are contested in each election.

The House of Representatives has 465 members. Of these, 289 are elected under a single-seat constituency system, while 176 are elected under a proportional representation system in which the nation is divided into 11 regions. The last general election was held in October 2021. The House of Councillors has 248 members, of whom 100 are elected through proportional representation, and 148 are elected as representatives from 45 electoral districts of the nation, based upon prefectures. The last regular election was held in July 2019.

In June 2015, revisions to the Public Offices Election Law, which consist mainly of lowering the voting age from 20 to 18 years or older, were established and promulgated. The revisions were applied starting with the House of Councillors regular election, which was officially announced in June 2016. Both men and women above the qualifying age are eligible to run in elections. The qualifying age for members of the House of

Representatives is 25 years or older, while the qualifying age for members of the House of Councillors is 30 years or older.

Table 17.1
Diet Members by Political Group

House of Representatives (as of April 28, 2022) Membership 465, Vacancies 0			House of Councillors (as of October 3, 2021) Membership [1] 245, Vacancies 3		
Name	Males	Females	Name	Males	Females
Incumbents	419	46	Incumbents	186	56
Liberal Democratic Party	243	20	Liberal Democratic Party and Voice of The People	94	17
The Constitutional Democratic Party of Japan and the Independent	84	13	The Constitutional Democratic Party of Japan and Social Democratic Party	30	15
Nippon Ishin (Japan Innovation Party)	37	4	Komeito	23	5
Komeito	28	4	Nippon Ishin (Japan Innovation Party)	12	3
Democratic Party For the People	10	1	Democratic Party For the People and The Shin-Ryokufukai	11	4
Japanese Communist Party	8	2	Japanese Communist Party	8	5
Yushi no Kai	5	0	Okinawa Whirlwind	2	0
REIWA SHINSENGUMI	1	2	REIWA SHINSENGUMI	1	1
			Hekisuikai	0	2
			Your Party	2	0
Independents	3	0	Independents	3	4

1) Due to the revision of the Public Offices Election Law in July 2018, the constant number of seats increased from 242 to 248. In the July 2019 regular election, half of this number, or 124 seats, were re-elected.

Source: The House of Representatives; The House of Councillors.

3. Executive Branch

The Cabinet exercises its executive power on the basis of the laws and budgets adopted by the Diet. The Cabinet, composed of the Prime Minister and other Ministers of State, is collectively responsible to the Diet, regarding the exercise of the executive power. The Prime Minister is elected in the Diet from among its members. The Ministers of State are appointed by the Prime Minister, and the majority of them must be Diet members. Thus, Japan adopts the parliamentary Cabinet system, in which the organization and existence of the Cabinet rest on the confidence in the Diet.

The Cabinet's powers include the following: (i) implementing laws; (ii) engaging in foreign diplomacy; (iii) signing treaties; (iv) overseeing the operational affairs of public officers; (v) formulating a budget and submitting it to the Diet; (vi) enacting Cabinet orders; and (vii) deciding amnesty. In addition, the Cabinet powers also include designating the Chief Justice of the Supreme Court and appointing other judges. The Cabinet also gives advice and approval to the Emperor in matters of state, and bears the responsibility for this.

Table 17.2
Successive Prime Ministers

Date [1]	Name	Date [1]	Name
Oct. 4, 2021	KISHIDA Fumio	Sep. 26, 2007	FUKUDA Yasuo
Sep. 16, 2020	SUGA Yoshihide	Sep. 26, 2006	ABE Shinzo
Dec. 26, 2012	ABE Shinzo	Apr. 26, 2001	KOIZUMI Junichiro
Sep. 2, 2011	NODA Yoshihiko	Apr. 5, 2000	MORI Yoshiro
Jun. 8, 2010	KAN Naoto	Jul. 30, 1998	OBUCHI Keizo
Sep. 16, 2009	HATOYAMA Yukio	Jan. 11, 1996	HASHIMOTO Ryutaro
Sep. 24, 2008	ASO Taro	Jun. 30, 1994	MURAYAMA Tomiichi

1) Date of initial cabinet formation.
Source: Prime Minister of Japan and His Cabinet.

4. Judicial Branch

Judicial power resides in the courts and is independent from the executive branch and the legislative branch.

The Constitution provides for the establishment of the Supreme Court as the highest court with final judgment, while the Court Act provides for 4 lower-level courts (High Court, District Court, Family Court and Summary Court). At present, there are 8 High Courts, 50 District Courts, 50 Family Courts, and 438 Summary Courts throughout the nation.

To ensure fair judgments, Japan uses a three-tiered judicial system. The first courts in the court hierarchy are the District Courts, the second are the High Courts, and the highest court is the Supreme Court. The system thus allows a case to be heard and ruled on up to 3 times in principle, should a party involved in the case so desire. The Summary Courts and Family Courts handle simple cases, domestic relations and cases involving juveniles as first courts.

The Supreme Court has the authority to deliver the final judgment on the legitimacy of any law, ordinance, regulation, or disposition. It is chaired by the Chief Justice and 14 judges.

A lay judge system began in May 2009. This is a system under which citizens participate in criminal trials as judges to determine, together with professional judges, whether the defendant is guilty or not and, if found guilty, what sentence should apply. What is hoped for is that the public's participation in criminal trials will make citizens feel more involved in the justice process and make the trials easier to understand, thus leading to the public's greater trust in the justice system. A total of 14,351 people were tried in lay judge trials held between the start of the system and December 2021.

Table 17.3
Judicial Cases Newly Commenced, Terminated or Pending (All courts)

(Thousands)

Year	Civil and administrative cases			Criminal cases [1]		
	Commenced	Terminated	Pending	Commenced	Terminated	Pending
2005	2,713	2,827	576	1,568	1,572	47
2010	2,179	2,241	536	1,158	1,161	36
2015	1,432	1,425	409	1,033	1,030	34
2019	1,523	1,509	430	885	885	31
2020	1,350	1,324	456	852	851	33

Year	Domestic cases			Juvenile cases [1]		
	Commenced	Terminated	Pending	Commenced	Terminated	Pending
2005	718	713	99	237	238	32
2010	815	815	106	165	168	25
2015	970	959	133	95	98	13
2019	1,092	1,082	146	58	58	9
2020	1,105	1,092	159	53	54	8

1) The number of persons.
Source: Supreme Court of Japan.

5. Local Governments

The affairs of local governments in Japan are conducted by ordinary local governments (prefectures and municipalities within each prefecture) and by special local governments, such as special wards. As of October 1, 2018, Japan has 47 prefectures, within which there are 1,718 municipalities, plus the 23 Cities of Tokyo metropolis. In order to strengthen the administrative and fiscal foundation of the municipalities, municipal mergers were promoted by law. Consequently, the number of municipalities was reduced by nearly half from the 3,232 existing at the end of March 1999.

Municipalities that satisfy certain population criteria (i.e., 500,000 people or more) are eligible for designation as "Ordinance-designated cities". This designation gives them administrative and fiscal authority equivalent to those of prefectures. With the addition of Kumamoto City in April 2012, there are presently 20 cities that have earned this designation. See the map on the inside back cover.

Figure 17.3
Government System by Level [1] (as of October 1, 2018)

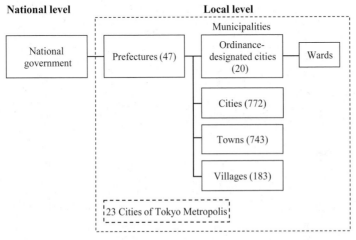

1) Figures in parentheses indicate number.
Source: Ministry of Internal Affairs and Communications.

Figure 17.4
Local Government Employees by Type of Administrative Services
(as of April 1, 2021)

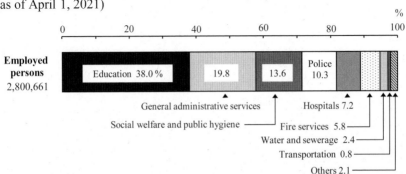

Source: Ministry of Internal Affairs and Communications.

Appendix 1
Population, Surface Area, and Population Density by Prefecture

Prefectures	Prefectural capital cities	Population (1,000)		Surface area (km²)		Population density (per km²)	
				Total area	Inhabitable	Total area	Inhabitable
		2020 [1]	2021 [2]	2020	2020	2019	2019
Japan		126,146	125,502	377,976	122,958	338	1,029
Hokkaido	Sapporo City	5,225	5,183	83,424	22,699	67	235
Aomori	Aomori City	1,238	1,221	9,646	3,253	129	386
Iwate	Morioka City	1,211	1,196	15,275	3,751	80	330
Miyagi	Sendai City	2,302	2,290	7,282	3,186	317	731
Akita	Akita City	960	945	11,638	3,233	83	302
Yamagata	Yamagata City	1,068	1,055	9,323	2,873	116	374
Fukushima	Fukushima City	1,833	1,812	13,784	4,231	134	438
Ibaraki	Mito City	2,867	2,852	6,097	3,889	469	719
Tochigi	Utsunomiya City	1,933	1,921	6,408	3,005	302	648
Gunma	Maebashi City	1,939	1,927	6,362	2,269	305	852
Saitama	Saitama City	7,345	7,340	3,798	2,603	1,935	2,844
Chiba	Chiba City	6,284	6,275	5,158	3,534	1,214	1,761
Tokyo	23 Cities of Tokyo	14,048	14,010	2,194	1,423	6,345	9,793
Kanagawa	Yokohama City	9,237	9,236	2,416	1,474	3,807	6,253
Niigata	Niigata City	2,201	2,177	12,584	4,550	177	490
Toyama	Toyama City	1,035	1,025	4,248	1,842	246	567
Ishikawa	Kanazawa City	1,133	1,125	4,186	1,395	272	818
Fukui	Fukui City	767	760	4,191	1,077	183	713
Yamanashi	Kofu City	810	805	4,465	953	182	850
Nagano	Nagano City	2,048	2,033	13,562	3,249	151	635
Gifu	Gifu City	1,979	1,961	10,621	2,211	187	899
Shizuoka	Shizuoka City	3,633	3,608	7,777	2,775	469	1,325
Aichi	Nagoya City	7,542	7,517	5,173	2,996	1,460	2,527
Mie	Tsu City	1,770	1,756	5,774	2,064	308	865
Shiga	Otsu City	1,414	1,411	4,017	1,300	352	1,082
Kyoto	Kyoto City	2,578	2,561	4,612	1,177	560	2,201
Osaka	Osaka City	8,838	8,806	1,905	1,334	4,623	6,620
Hyogo	Kobe City	5,465	5,432	8,401	2,770	651	1,964
Nara	Nara City	1,324	1,315	3,691	854	360	1,555
Wakayama	Wakayama City	923	914	4,725	1,123	196	830
Tottori	Tottori City	553	549	3,507	904	159	617
Shimane	Matsue City	671	665	6,708	1,271	101	519
Okayama	Okayama City	1,888	1,876	7,114	2,228	266	852
Hiroshima	Hiroshima City	2,800	2,780	8,480	2,299	331	1,213
Yamaguchi	Yamaguchi City	1,342	1,328	6,113	1,715	222	796
Tokushima	Tokushima City	720	712	4,147	1,016	176	721
Kagawa	Takamatsu City	950	942	1,877	1,005	509	951
Ehime	Matsuyama City	1,335	1,321	5,676	1,666	236	800
Kochi	Kochi City	692	684	7,104	1,161	98	600
Fukuoka	Fukuoka City	5,135	5,124	4,987	2,763	1,024	1,848
Saga	Saga City	811	806	2,441	1,335	334	610
Nagasaki	Nagasaki City	1,312	1,297	4,131	1,668	321	792
Kumamoto	Kumamoto City	1,738	1,728	7,409	2,747	236	625
Oita	Oita City	1,124	1,114	6,341	1,795	179	631
Miyazaki	Miyazaki City	1,070	1,061	7,735	1,876	139	580
Kagoshima	Kagoshima City	1,588	1,576	9,187	3,288	174	484
Okinawa	Naha City	1,467	1,468	2,283	1,127	637	1,243

1) Population Census. 2) Population Estimates.
Source: Statistics Bureau, MIC; Geospatial Information Authority of Japan.

Appendix 2
Conversion Factors

	Metric units	British Imperial and U.S. equivalents	
Length:	1 centimeter (cm)	0.39370	inches
	1 meter (m) .... {	3.28084	feet
		1.09361	yards
	1 kilometer (km)	0.62137	miles
Area:	1 square meter (m^2) .... {	10.76392	square feet
		1.19599	square yards
	1 square kilometer (km^2)	0.38610	square miles
	1 hectare (ha) 10,000 square meters (m^2) }	2.47105	acres
Volume:	1 cubic meter (m^3) .... {	35.31472	cubic feet
		1.30795	cubic yards
Weight:	1 kilogram (kg) .... {	35.27399	ounces
		2.20462	pounds
	1 ton (t) .... {	0.98421	long tons
		1.10231	short tons
Capacity:	1 liter (L) .... {	0.87988	imp. Quarts
		1.05669	U.S. liq. Quarts
Temperature:	centigrade (°C)	5 / 9 ×(Fahrenheit - 32)	

Appendix 3
Foreign Exchange Rates [1]

(Yen per U.S. dollar)

Year	Average	End of year
2000	107.77	114.90
2001	121.53	131.47
2002	125.31	119.37
2003	115.93	106.97
2004	108.18	103.78
2005	110.16	117.48
2006	116.31	118.92
2007	117.76	113.12
2008	103.37	90.28
2009	93.54	92.13
2010	87.78	81.51
2011	79.81	77.57
2012	79.81	86.32
2013	97.63	105.37
2014	105.85	119.80
2015	121.03	120.42
2016	108.84	117.11
2017	112.16	112.65
2018	110.39	110.40
2019	109.01	109.15
2020	106.78	103.33
2021	109.80	115.12

1) Midpoint rate in the interbank foreign exchange market in Tokyo.
Source: Bank of Japan.

Statistical Information in English

Publication

Japan Statistical Yearbook

This is the most comprehensive statistical publication on Japan, covering a broad range of fields including land, population, economy, society, culture, etc. The recent issue contains about 540 tables.

To purchase a copy, please contact:
Official Gazette Co-operation of Japan
Tel: +81-3-6737-1506
E-mail: overseas@gov-book.or.jp
https://www.gov-book.or.jp/en/
Japan Statistical Association (Shipment inside Japan only)
Tel: +81-3-5332-3151
E-mail: jsa@jstat.or.jp
https://www.jstat.or.jp/

Statistics Bureau website
https://www.stat.go.jp/english/index.html

This website provides a variety of statistical information on Japan.

Japan Statistical Yearbook

Web version of the above yearbook.

Statistics Bureau
Ministry of Internal Affairs and Communications
Japan

Administrative Map of Japan (As of April 1, 2022)

Japan is divided into 47 prefectures.

The words printed in black are the names of 47 prefectures and those printed in blue italics are the names of prefectural capital cities and/or Ordinance-designated cities.

- ○ Prefectural capital cities
- ● Prefectural capital cities (also Ordinance-designated cities)
- ▲ Ordinance-designated cities

Fukuoka City
Kitakyushu City
Saga City
Saga
Fukuoka
Nagasaki
Nagasaki City
Kumamoto City
Oita
Kumamoto
Oita City
Yamaguchi
Yamaguchi City
Miyazaki
Kagoshima City
Miyazaki City
Kagoshima

Matsue City
Shimane
Hiroshima
Hiroshima City
Okayama
Okayama City
Matsuyama City
Ehime
Kochi City
Kochi

Tottori City
Sakai City
Osaka City
Tottori
Fukui
Kyoto City
Kyoto
Shiga
Otsu C
Nara City
Tsu Ci
Mie
Hyogo
Kagawa
Takamatsu City
Kobe City
Tokushima
Tokushima City
Osaka
Wakayama City
Nara
Wakayama

1 : 7,273,000

0   100   200